Growth and Integration in Central America

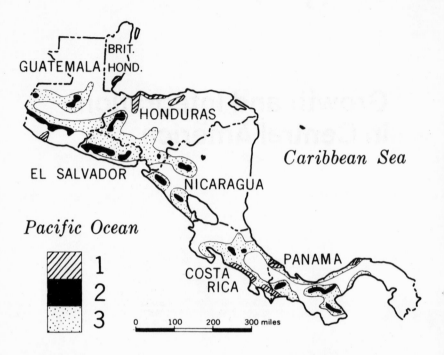

Major areas of production: 1—bananas; 2—coffee; 3—corn and other subsistence crops

PRAEGER SPECIAL STUDIES IN
INTERNATIONAL ECONOMICS AND DEVELOPMENT

Growth and Integration in Central America

Carlos M. Castillo

FREDERICK A. PRAEGER, Publishers
New York · Washington · London

The purpose of the Praeger Special Studies is to make specialized research monographs in U.S. and international economics and politics available to the academic, business, and government communities. For further information, write to the Special Projects Division, Frederick A. Praeger, Publishers, 111 Fourth Avenue, New York, N.Y. 10003.

FREDERICK A. PRAEGER, PUBLISHERS
111 Fourth Avenue, New York, N.Y. 10003, U.S.A.
77-79 Charlotte Street, London W.1, England

Published in the United States of America in 1966
by Frederick A. Praeger, Inc., Publishers

Library of Congress Catalog Card Number: 66-18896

Printed in the United States of America

PREFACE

This is a study in economic organization. It deals with issues of construction and reconstruction of small economic systems, namely those of the Central American countries: Guatemala, El Salvador, Honduras, Nicaragua and Costa Rica.

The study is based upon the experience gained over several years of work in the Central American program for economic integration. It grows out of an inquiry into the working and operations of public policy, as expressed in the actions taken by five governments during more than one decade, with a view to creating conditions for rapid and sustained development, through the transformation of five national systems into a single economy of regional scope. Although a large part of the study is devoted to an interpretation of these countries' economic history and to an analysis of the nature and significance of their movement toward integration, the main concern is with the problems of the future, and in particular, with the ways in which the methods and approaches that have produced successful results in the past may be used to bring about and consolidate that transformation.

Much time was spent, prior to 1964, sharpening the conceptual elements underlying this work and gathering, selecting and testing the required empirical materials; most of the writing was done during the summer of that year at the main campus of The University of Wisconsin in Madison. This would not have been possible without the generous co-operation and facilities provided by the Land Tenure Center and the continuous help and encouragement of all of its staff in residence there.

The work done, in whatever merits it may have, owes a large debt to many friends and professional colleagues. It is difficult to mention all of them. But it is only fair to acknowledge the invaluable contributions made by Professors Kenneth H. Parsons, Raymond J. Penn and Carl Bogholt, of The University of Wisconsin, and Erven J. Long, formerly of The University of Tennessee, from the standpoint of the theory of inquiry and the theory of economic policy; and by Mr. Cristobal Lara Beautell, formerly of the United Nations Economic Commission for Latin America, in connection with the substantive problems of economic integration and the role of the economist in the policy making process. Two colleagues at the United Nations Economic Commission for Latin America gave generously of their time to improve

255122

the initial drafts: Mr. David Ibarra helped greatly from the standpoint of rigor and precision of analysis on points which were inadequately formulated at first; Mr. Joseph Moscarella contributed in removing the imperfections of the original text for final publication; and, in so doing, illuminated many matters of substance. The writer wishes to express to all of them his sincere gratitude for their help and, more generally, for the academic and professional association which it has been his good fortune to enjoy with them over many years.

Because of his deep personal and professional involvement in the Central American economic integration program, it would be somewhat idle for the writer to claim complete objectivity in this study. He dares to hope, however, that it is the result of a detached effort to examine the problems under investigation in the perspective afforded by the use of techniques of inquiry which proceed in terms of an analysis of the consequences arising from particular governmental actions, and not from the subjective positions that might develop with reference to small interests or short-lived urgencies.

Although the author is an official of the United Nations Economic Commission for Latin America (ECLA), he has written this study in his personal capacity. It will be found that nothing is said in the text by way of evaluation of the role played by ECLA in the integration program during the period under study. It remains for others to determine what this role may have been.

Mexico City, June 1966.

CONTENTS

PART I

THE DEVELOPMENT OF THE EXPORT ECONOMY

CHAPTER **1** DISINTEGRATION OF THE
FEDERAL REPUBLIC: ITS
POLITICAL AND ECONOMIC
BASES

The Background of Colonial Administration

Central America was organized as a federal republic, when it
obtained its independence from Spain in 1821, and comprised the
provinces and other territorial units of the old Capitanía General de
Guatemala of colonial times. This federal unit was a nominal rather
than a real fact. It soon became apparent that the political and
economic bases for a cohesive national organization of Central
American scope were lacking, and that the existence of a unified
entity in the colony had been made possible largely by the operation
of an external prerogative.

Even the unity of the Capitanía General is a questionable fact,
as some features of the political, administrative and religious organization made instead for its segmentation. The lack of correspondence
between the territorial units of the government and those of the church
was important since the latter was in charge of certain judicial
functions. For several decades, around the middle of the eighteenth
century, the central bodies of political and judicial administration
were located in different places.

Contradictory policies were often followed in the appointment of
high level officials. Although the provincial governors were under
the jurisdiction of the Captain General, some of them were appointed
directly by the King; still others, including the governors of certain
ports, were appointed by the King and were responsible directly to
the Crown. The heads of the smaller jurisdictions within the
provinces were generally under the authority of the provincial

governors, but some of them operated directly under the Captain
General. The municipal authorities were not appointed but rather
were elected by the citizens.[1]

Having a geographic environment which made unity difficult,
with the further handicap of difficult transportation and communications, it is easy to see how this mosaic of unrelated and frequently
contradictory centers of authority tended to strengthen instead of
to overcome the region's fragmentation. The disappearance of Spanish
colonial rule brought the resulting characteristics to the surface in
sharp relief. By 1840, this combination of forces had already resulted
in the disintegration of the federal republic. It should be noted that
this type of centrifugal process, emerging upon the achievement of
political independence, is a well established fact in the political and
economic evolution of colonial areas, and is by no means characteristic only of Central America.[2]

The Economic Basis of Fragmentation

The several territorial components of the Capitanía General had
remained in permanent economic isolation from each other. This is
generally attributed to the lack of adequate means of transport and
communication and to the large subsistence elements in the economies
of the region. But the argument is redundant, for these obstacles to
internal trade could have been overcome with time. The permanence
of an internally fragmented system is to be ascribed rather to the
economic policy followed by colonial authorities.

The primary and almost exclusive objective of colonial policy was
to develop and maintain reciprocal trade flows between the center
overseas and each of the individual provinces. The movement of goods
on an   intraregional basis was discouraged by high internal duties.
Also,from province to province the regional authority was used to
prevent local production for shipment among them. For example,
trade between Costa Rica and Panama was forbidden, allegedly on the
grounds that it was the way to clamp down on smuggling from Jamaica.[3]
The cattle trade which took place between Honduras and Guatemala
and which has persisted up to the present, was one of the few
exceptions, but it was stymied by the exploitative practices exercised
by importers in Guatemala upon Honduran producers.

In this case colonial policy was applied to a group of relatively poor enclaves of the Spanish Crown, by comparison with most of the rest of the Western Hemisphere colonies. Although gold and silver constituted two of their main exports, principally from the Honduran mines, their mineral resources were small in relation to those of Peru or Mexico. Their productive activities were mostly agricultural, with large elements of subsistence farming. Cacao, hides and tallow, indigo and cotton were among the agricultural commodities entering the region's small exports.

Foreign trade was conducted mostly with Spain and had to face great difficulties. Business could be transacted with relative freedom only in one market. But access even to this market was restricted, as very few local ports were legally authorized to engage in foreign trade, while goods could be shipped to one or two Spanish ports only. Moreover, this access was uncertain and irregular, since the Central American provinces were far removed from the main lines of inter-continental transportation.

There were also difficulties on the supply side: Knowledge was lacking about techniques of mineral and agricultural production for export; taxes were high; imports of inputs and of consumer articles were frequently short, and state monopolies controlled production of some goods.

The growing competition for world supremacy among Spain, Great Britain and France made the situation still more difficult, when the struggle was carried to the outer Caribbean during the eighteenth century.[4] An acute shortage of transportation facilities developed for Central American foreign trade upon the exclusion of Panama as one of the main centers for the routing of Spanish ships. Located near the sea, production of such export commodities as cacao was disrupted and brought practically to an end, as a result of increasingly frequent pirate raids along the shores of the Isthmus. In turn, the normal conduct of import trade suffered from sizable smuggling operations from Belize, Jamaica and the Island of Guadeloupe.

Efforts toward a greater degree of autonomy from Spanish rule, beginning around 1810, were stimulated by the combined effects of all of these factors. Successful on that count, when independence came these countries had been undergoing a substantial economic decline for several decades and found themselves with the main commercially productive activities largely paralyzed.[5]

Under these conditions, there were few possibilities in 1821 for the Central American provinces to trade among themselves. In addition, the very high transportation costs were practically insurmountable, and the basic fact remained that they had been developed as self-contained compartments, each producing the same commodities, each providing for its own needs, all having the same type of relationship with the outside world, as regards markets, import requirements and export possibilities. From the economic point of view, therefore, there was no basis for them to organize a viable federal republic.

Drastic changes in trade policy followed the attainment of independence. Henceforth, free trade with the rest of the world prevailed without any limitations as to ports, countries or commodities. This change, and this change alone, seems to have been responsible for the very rapid recovery of foreign trade between 1821 and 1825. In spite of the initially critical conditions, productive activities reacted very quickly to the stimulus of renewed contacts with foreign markets. Exports of goods doubled in those four years. This gives an idea as to the amount of productive capacity which was idle previously.[6] Imports also increased rapidly, and provided a long awaited improvement in the patterns of consumption of the population.

Operation of Centrifugal Forces in the Newly Independent Economies

The tendency toward increased ties with the outside world did not make for the strengthening of the federal republic. Centrifugal forces were released by the way in which the resurgence of foreign trade took place, superimposing themselves upon mutually competitive productive structures and the existing obstacles to regional transportation. The growth of foreign trade itself did not promote the breakdown of the federal unit. Its role in such a breakdown was due rather to the fact that the corresponding governmental functions were fulfilled at the provincial level, so that there were five different outward processes taking place at the same time instead of one, responding to five different centers of authority.

The Republic of Central America was never in a position to fulfill the real and essential functions of government, as distinguished from the purely formal ones. In the anti-Spanish reaction that followed upon the attainment of independence, the federal administration deprived itself of the main sources of revenues by eliminating taxes that had long been a source of friction with colonial authorities. State governments retained the vital function of collecting and pro- viding revenues to the federation.[7]

The development of a political and economic unit of genuinely Central American dimensions required, among other things, the establishment of a strong federal fiscal system. Based upon a regional customs organization and a regional institution to collect revenues from state monopolies belonging to the federation, such a system could have perhaps gone a long way in tapping the foreign trade upsurge as a source of strength for the young republic. Perhaps. The fact is, however, that no action was taken to turn the economic tide in this direction.

The Political Process of Disintegration

Political forces were working together with the economic factors and against the continued existence of the federation. A localism, with close and direct relationships to the economic realities mentioned above, has always been one of the biggest obstacles in the construction of a national point of view in Central America. Not only was this phenomenon to play an important role in the breakdown of the federal republic, but later on it was to be utilized by foreign powers to promote their own political and economic interests.

Localism engendered "caudillismo," one of Latin America's endemic political diseases, and thus threatened the stability of the federal system almost from the beginning. The corrosive effects were compounded in this case by the secular resentment in the provinces against Guatemala, the seat of colonial rule, accumulated because of its disproportionately larger political and economic influence and of the exploitative practices of the government in the fields of trade and taxation. This resentment does not seem to have diminished with the advent of independence, due to the centralist and monopolistic tendencies of the more powerful conservative Guatemalan groups.[8]

The conflict between liberalism and conservatism, which domi- nated the scene well into the second half of the nineteenth century, strengthened these conflicts and contributed to the disintegration of the federal republic.[9] The influence of the French and of the American revolutions had already been felt in Central America before its inde- pendence. After 1821, the typical conflicts between republicanism

and monarchism, church and state, democracy and aristocracy exerted
a powerful and divisive influence on the young and weak federation.

Liberalism and localism were directly related, as the democratic
impulses came from the provinces and the municipalities. They both
supported a federalist republic, against the threat of centralism posed
by the conservatives in the seat of the federal government, as in
1826-29. Subsequently, however, liberals in the provinces parted
company with those in Guatemala City and followed the lines of
localism, while the policies of the center continued to add to the long
standing provincial resentment. The situation was further complicated
by the seething conflict in the Capital between the liberals in the
federal government and the conservative powers of the State of
Guatemala.[10]

These tensions led to frequent uprisings and to a practically
permanent military strife throughout most of the region. The para-
lysing effect of such a situation was very great, as economic activity
could not unfold in an appropriate environment. With the consequent
shrinking of the regular sources of government, financing extraordinary
(forced) levies were imposed, which contributed further to economic
stagnation, since their proceeds were utilized for military activities
rather than public services and productive investment.

The conservative victory of the late 1830's in Guatemala brought
the federal republic to its end, as the struggle with the provincial
liberals had forced the conservatives to replace their centralism with
a separatist position.[11]

Thereafter, the conflict between the two political groupings
shifted to the national level and gave rise to armed incursions against
one another, especially in Guatemala, El Salvador and Honduras. In
this way, new strenghth was given to the continuing phenomena of
localism and "caudillismo," throughout the area.

External Factors: The Struggle for Control of
Interoceanic Communications

It is therefore understandable that both the concept and the fact
of a united Central America should have collapsed as a result of the
interaction of such economic and political factors. External pressures
also added to internal instability and limited the possibilities of giving

new orientation to the economic development of the region for several decades, particularly in the normal dealings with the then main centers of international trade. One of the more important concerns of the Central American countries in this period was that of coping with the danger of losing their political independence at the hands of some foreign power. The following experiences attest to the reality of this danger: The long time British occupation of portions of the Atlantic coast in Nicaragua and Honduras--the so-called protectorate of the Mosquitia--; the American filibuster invasion of Nicaragua and Costa Rica of 1855-57, effected with the aid of some of what were soon to become the Confederate States; the British blockade and bombardment of Central American ports in Honduras and El Salvador on several occasions; the British threat of invasion in Nicaragua around 1895 and the American occupation of this country beginning in 1910. Such instances are mentioned here by way of illustration, and do not include all kinds and manners of chronic minor interventions by the two powers in the internal political affairs of these countries. On March 20, 1850, for example, the Vice-Admiral and Commander of the British Naval forces in the Caribbean threatened to blockade and, if necessary, to bombard the ports of El Salvador, unless the government of that country complied immediately with an agreement signed on November 12, 1849. One of the claims at stake was the reimbursement to a British subject of a 244 pesos duty on certain goods which he had imported eight years before, in 1841, and which in the view of the British government should not have been paid.[12]

The source of the predicament in which Central America found herself was not the attraction of her natural resources, which did not offer particularly interesting prospects to foreign investment; it was rather the value of the Isthmus as a potential route for interoceanic transportation and communication.[13] The canal was finally built in Panama, but in earlier times the utilization of the San Juan river and Lake Nicaragua for this purpose appeared as a prominent possibility. In fact, many people took the Nicaraguan route during the gold rush-- using the wagons and small boat facilities of Cornelius Vanderbilt's "Compañía del Tránsito"[14]--to travel back and forth between California and the Atlantic coast of the United States.

The question of the control of the area gave rise to a protracted conflict between the United States and Great Britain, during the latter half of the nineteenth century. The internal conflict over slavery, which was to lead to the Civil War in the United States, and the likelihood of war between Great Britain and Russia over the spoils of

the Ottoman Empire, respectively, prevented the two powers from military conflict over this issue. A modus vivendi was reached in 1850 by
means of the Clayton-Bulver Treaty.[15] This contributed in no small
measure to the continued existence of the Central American countries
as independent entities. It was not until then that they began to
emerge in the modern international economy.

The issue was finally settled in favor of the United States around
the turn of this century, with the United Kingdom giving up its claims
to the interoceanic waterway in the Hay-Paucefote Treaty signed in
Washington, on December 18, 1901.[16] The Treaty in effect ratified the
fact that Central America and the Caribbean had slowly but surely
come to be a zone of United States political and economic influence.

This fact has imposed severe limitations on the degree of sovereignty enjoyed by the five republics. However, the resulting
influence has not precluded either the formal recognition of their
political individuality or the actual exercise of a measure of relative
independence. Among other things, it permitted the development of
an export economy largely of their own, which was to be the mainstay
of their economic growth over the next fifty to seventy five years.

Footnotes to Chapter 1

1. Rodrigo Facio, Trayectoria y Crisis de la Federación Centroamericana (San José, Costa Rica: Imprenta Nacional, 1949),
pp. 12-21.

2. See, for example, J. S. Furnivall, Colonial Policy and
Practice (Cambridge: Cambridge University Press, 1948), and
C. M. Castillo, "Problemas Políticos y Administrativos del Desarrollo
Económico," El Trimestre Económico (Mexico City: Fondo de Cultura
Económica, 1960), Vol. XXVI (1) No. 101, p. 54.

3. Tomás Soley Güell, Historia Económica y Hacendaria de
Costa Rica (San José, Costa Rica: Editorial Universitaria, 1947),
Vol. I, p. 115, and León Fernández, Documentos para la historia de
Costa Rica, quoted by Rodrigo Facio, op. cit., p. 28.

4. Celso Furtado, Formación Económica del Brasil (Mexico City:
Fondo de Cultura Económica, 1962), pp. 27-39.

5. For the empirical basis of the interpretation contained herein and for extended accounts of the economic processes in colonial Central America, see Valentín Solórzano Fernández, Historia de la Evolución Económica de Guatemala (Mexico City, 1947), pp.113-194, 211-212; Soley Güell, op. cit., Vol. I, pp. 45-116, and Facio, op. cit., pp. 21-35.

6. Solórzano Fernández, op. cit., pp. 243-246.

7. Soley Güell, op. cit., pp. 144-45. Thomas L. Karnes, The Failure of Union: Central America (Chapel Hill, N. C.: The University of North Carolina Press, 1961), pp. 58-59, 77.

8. See Karnes, op. cit., Chapters I-IV, for an informative account of attitudes toward Guatemala before and after independence.

9. Facio, op. cit., pp. 75-85.

10. Enrique Guier, El General Morazán (San José, Costa Rica: Imprenta Lehmann, 1962).

11. Abelardo Torres, Evolución de las ideas liberales en las Instituciones Políticas y Jurídicas de la República Federal de Centro-américa y del Estado de El Salvador (San Salvador: University of El Salvador, 1951), pp. 112-114. /Mimeographed/.

12. Francisco J. Monterrey, Historia de El Salvador (San Salvador, 1943), pp. 334-335.

13. Albert Z. Carr, The World and William Walker (New York: Harper and Row, 1963), pp. 42-55.

14. Rafael Obregón Loría, La Campaña del Tránsito (San José, Costa Rica: Editorial Universitaria, 1956).

15. Carr, op. cit., pp. 50-55; Vicente Sáenz, Nuestras Vías Interocéanicas (Mexico City: Editorial América Nueva, 1957), pp. 155-160.

16. Sáenz, ibid., pp. 171-173.

2

DEVELOPMENT OF THE CENTRAL AMERICAN ECONOMIES

Growing Limitations of the Colonial Economy after Independence

Consonant with the experience throughout many other areas, the history of Central American development is the history of the outward growth of an agricultural export economy. These countries began to emerge in the modern world as their productive activity turned to new geographic and commodity markets. Within the liberal commercial policy adopted after becoming independent of Spanish rule, Great Britain, France, Germany and the United States began to influence the region's trade in new directions. Cochineal developed as an important source of foreign exchange and, together with indigo, cacao and gold and silver, constituted the core of the export sector.[1]

This productive structure, however, was not a source of sustained economic growth. The production of gold and silver increased slowly because of comparatively low yields and high costs of extraction. Output of indigo and cochineal declined, as a result of disease and other natural causes and of the shift of the European textile industries to the new chemical dyes originally developed in Germany.

It was not until the middle of the nineteenth century that the long search for substantial export lines came to a successful end in Central America.[2] From then on, and for the next one hundred years, the agricultural export economy was to be based upon the production of coffee and bananas.

Political and Legal Changes in the Development
of New Agricultural Exports

The enlargement of the available market through international trade and the growing demand for a commodity which was particularly adapted to the capabilities of the region's resources, opened up unprecedented possibilities for economic gain. Coffee production started to increase in the several countries at different times during the second half of the century, and by 1900 it had become their main export.

The organization of an efficient export economy, capable of fully exploiting the new opportunities open to the five countries, required the creation of certain conditions and the solution of several problems. Among such conditions, the establishment of a minimum of order and the consolidation of national governments were essential. This resulted in no small measure from the termination of civil strife among the countries on the issue of federalism, with the breakdown of the Central American Republic; it was also aided by their successful fight against foreign invasion in 1856-57 and by the British-American détente on the question of interoceanic communications. It then became possible for Central Americans to concentrate on the development of their productive potential within the framework of the present five national units.

The growth of the new export activities found important obstacles in the existing institutions and forms of economic organization. These obstacles arose at various strategic points: The credit system, the land tenure system, and the economic power of the Church. It was difficult to utilize property in land as security for loans, and large tracts belonged to the towns and were not subject to private ownership. The clergy controlled sizable amounts of wealth and syphoned off a substantial fraction of the income of the population,[3] while the traditional merchants and real estate owners dominated much of the rest of the economic power structure.[4]

The emergence of liberalism as the moving force in the affairs of these countries provided both the philosophy and the means to solve these problems and to construct a new system of economic opportunity, where there were only a few physical possibilities. It sanctioned the quest for profit and gave rise to a legal reform of far-reaching consequences. During the second half of the nineteenth century the Central American countries adopted new civil legislation, fashioning their laws of property after the French Civil Code. These and other measures made for the secularization of Church properties, provided for the conversion of the still existing communal properties into the system of private ownership, and facilitated the development of credit for the new agricultural export activities.[5]

In this way, a throughgoing reorganization of control over land and human resources, and a radical reorientation of the uses to which they could be put, were made possible. A new set of land tenure and farm labor arrangements came into existence with the modern commercial plantation, which provided the legal and institutional framework for both the acquisition of the required technologies and for the quick expansion of coffee production and exports.[6]

Thus the liberal-conservative battle was fought also in the newly formed countries, the former states of the federal republic. It was not simply a conflict of ideological views, for powerful economic interests were also at stake. It was among the disaffected groups, in the ranks of the export producers, bankers, shippers and exporters, that the liberal intellectuals found some of their more effective supporters. And it was their combined efforts which brought victory to liberalism in the five countries between 1870 and 1895.

The new group of coffee growers moved into the higher layers of the economic power structure, aided by direct subsidies, tax exemptions, land grants and public technical assistance,[7] in addition to the major reforms introduced in the laws of property and credit. This group, which in time became solidified into a new social class, was made up of the victorious liberals and their sons and absorbed in its ranks the influx of German immigrants,--particularly in Guatemala --who had left their motherland during the revolution of 1848, and later, when the German national government superseded the princely states.[8]

The Construction of an Economic Infrastructure

The growth of Central America's foreign trade was hampered at first not only by institutional and organizational problems, but also by the lack of modern means of transportation and communication. Internal transportation from the production areas inland to the sea was costly and undependable, while the absence of port facilities on the Atlantic coast made it necessary to ship via the longer and more expensive Pacific routes.

The development of roads, railroads,and port facilities was fixed as a primary objective of public policy since early in the independent life of these countries. For several decades this resulted in a series of unsuccessful efforts, frustrated attempts to obtain external financing, and unfulfilled contracts with private parties for the construction of the required public works in exchange for land grants, monopoly franchises and other state privileges. It was not until the last quarter of the century that the building of railroads and the improvement of port facilities were achieved.

The success of this process was closely interrelated with the development of banana production as the second chief line of exports. The introduction of that productive activity after 1870, with its exacting requirements for rapid transportation and shipping facilities, performed a stimulating role in the successful completion of various public investment projects. To a large extent, the availability of ocean shipping facilities and the construction of radio communications may be traced directly to the requirements of this industry and to the action of the respective foreign corporations to fulfill them. In Costa Rica and Honduras, for example, the railroads grew hand in hand with the culti-vation of bananas. In these two countries, as well as in Guatemala, this commodity provided, together with coffee and imports, the mini-mum volume of traffic necessary for an economic operation of the railroads.[9]

The rise of a new economic class, the establishment of an appropri-ate legal and institutional framework for the development of economic activity,and the construction of the basic works of an economic infra-structure facilitated the expansion of the export economy in the Central American countries at an accelerated rate. On the basis of indirect information it may be estimated that coffee output increased about 45 per cent from 1865 to 1885, whereas between 1885 and 1905 these exports more than doubled, from 42.8 to 88.8 thousand tons yearly.[10]

The growth of banana exports took place at a much faster rate. The volume of shipments for Central America as a whole, which in 1900 was recorded at 9.5 million stems, increased almost fourfold during the next twenty five years having reached 37.4 million stems annually during the five year period 1925-29.[11] These results were achieved by foreign corporate firms, aided by land grants and other governmental incentives, as well as by ample investment funds from the outside and the modern techniques of agricultural production, including the eradication of endemic disease. Economic life was brought to areas reclaimed from swamps, malaria, and the tropical jungle. Modern, large scale plantations were set up, and large groups of the population were organized into a labor force that had to perform in accordance with the complex production and shipping requirements of a highly perishable commodity.[12]

Broader Implications of the Growth Process

The significance of the development of an export economy went far beyond the changes in resource use, the direction of trade and the emergence of new commodity markets: It was part and parcel of the process of articulation of the Central American nationalities, which in large measure superseded their traditional localism. In addition to the rise in the volume of exports and to the related changes in the organization of agriculture, some access was gained to the capital markets in England and France.[13] Several public investment projects were financed through government borrowing in these markets. Foreign lending institutions also financed private investments in the coffee industry, mainly those in processing facilities. Direct foreign investment, which had concentrated earlier exclusively in mining, was extended in considerably larger proportions to the banana industry, port facilities, railroads and communication centers.

The rise of exports made possible the development of a growing import trade. Manufactured consumer goods became available to larger segments of the population and changes of an appreciable magnitude took place in the patterns of consumption, both from the standpoint of their composition and of their differentiation among income groups. Purchases of capital goods, new building materials, and agricultural tools and implements also increased. Banking institutions--some of them foreign--were established to fulfill the credit needs of this trade as well as that of exports. Up to fairly recent times, for example, short-term production credit for coffee came mostly from foreign-owned banks and trading firms.

All of this added important commercial dimensions to economic activity and was at the core of the process of monetization of the economic system, as well as of a certain degree of urbanization of social life. In time, the monetary sector was tied--although pre-cariously--to the gold standard,[14] and the numbers of people living in cities--mainly in the capitals--increased to proportions previously unexperienced.

The development of new economic activities and their orientation toward external markets, as well as the increasing populations of the capital cities and the growing concentration of rural people in plantations, strengthened the position of the central national administrations, at the expense of lesser jurisdictions, and determined the need for new and expanded governmental functions. These functions made for a higher order of complexity in the governmental structure, particularly in such fields as customs administration, tax collection, the national military establishment, public works and the judiciary. Through these means, and within the framework of a power structure dominated by coffee growers and import merchants, the orientation of the political system came to respond to a public policy which was geared to the interests and necessities of an outward process of economic growth.

To be sure, not everything was of a positive nature in this process. As will be seen in the following chapters, internal limitations soon became apparent in the new productive structures. Here we may note some of the problems that arose in connection with the peculiar role played by foreign investment, and more generally, with the kind of relationships established with the external financial world.

As previously indicated, foreign direct investments and, to a lesser extent, foreign loans were decisive factors in the development of the Central American economies. But their costs were high, even by the standards then prevailing in the more advanced countries. In particular, the foreign borrowing experiences were not happy ones from the very start.

In spite of repeated efforts, none of the countries succeeded in having access to the international financial markets until late in the nineteenth century.[15] The conditions of the first loans were so onerous, as regards interest, repayment, bankers' commissions and discounts upon issue, that the governments concerned received only a fraction of their nominal values and were unable to carry out the projects for which they were intended. Thus, to cite a typical example, the government of Costa Rica received only £ 900,000 out of the two loans raised in London in 1871, with a total nominal value of £ 3.4 million.[16] The experience was similar in the other countries, particularly Honduras, which had raised four sterling loans totalling about £ 6.1 million between 1867 and 1870, for the construction of an interoceanic railway. Only a small section was built, however; and to this day the capital of this country is not connected by rail to its seaports.

Nearly all of these early loans went into default, and the subsequent foreign borrowing operations of the various countries were
devoted mainly to their conversion, the funding of accumulated
arrears of interest and the repayment of internal debts. Some countries,
notably Costa Rica and Guatemala, succeeded in obtaining additional
loans for financing new ventures during the first quarter of this
century. But on the whole, foreign borrowing was not an important
source of finance for public investment in Central America, as was the
case in Mexico and in some of the larger countries of South America.

As already noted, one important consequence of this was that the
governments were forced to rely heavily on the foreign companies and
their subsidiaries for the completion or the construction of railways,
ports and communications facilities, in exchange for generous
concessions under long-term contracts, usually ranging up to
ninety-nine years in duration. These contracts, as well as those
granted later to the American and Canadian electric power companies,
contained liberal terms regarding the provision of the services and
facilities concerned, particularly with respect to the regulation of
rates, which were generally set at high levels, in order to permit
rapid recovery of the initial investments.

In addition, some contracts provided for substantial land grants,
as well as exemptions from all existing and future taxes, other than
those specified therein.[17] Until 1948-50, when the tax clauses of the
original contracts were renegotiated, the fruit companies paid no tax
on their profits, and were subject only to a small par quantum tax on
banana exports, import duties on consumer goods for resale to their
employees, and minor taxes on property not directly related to their
production and shipping activities.

These experiences cannot be associated with any given cause;
they reflect rather a whole host of factors that have conditioned the
region's economic relations with the outside world. The much greater
strength of foreign interests--ultimately supported by their respective
governments--relative to that of the Central American countries;
a marked inability of the latter to operate efficiently in the international sphere; the substantial risks and other costs involved in the
transfer of external funds to the region, and sometimes their partial
diversion to private ends rather than public purposes, are among the
factors that should be studied in any analysis of the problem.

It can be argued that the costs of foreign investments were not higher in Central America than in other regions of the world periphery. But there is little doubt that they were high in the sense that much of the increase in production and productivity of the export sector was channeled to the servicing of the corresponding foreign investments. Thus, the share available for further economic expansion was reduced to relatively small proportions. Moreover, the production and investment policies of the foreign corporate firms in the area were geared to the more global strategies of the mother companies abroad, which did not necessarily coincide with the needs for additional development of the countries themselves.

The influence of the foreign enterprises went beyond the economic sphere. Given the region's political fragmentation, it was not diffi-cult, by playing upon the rivalries between countries and between factions in each country, to exert effective pressures on the behavior of the respective governments. The process was further aided by the latters' almost chronic dependence on loans or advance tax payments in order to meet urgent fiscal needs. All this tended to add to the causes of political instability, which facilitated the adaptation in varying degrees of the functions of government to the requirements of the external interests involved.

Out of this adaptation, and in response to other external and internal factors, there gradually emerged the now familiar inertia of the monocultural economy that has limited the horizon of possibilities for the expansion and diversification of the productive structures of the region. In addition, the stresses resulting from the shift of large labor groups from traditional agriculture to the more complex environ-ments of the modern corporate plantation, sowed the seeds for what later were to become some of the more serious social problems in Central America.

The Varying Experiences of Individual Countries

The general outline of the pattern of development of the export economy in Central America that has been sketched above overlooks the differences that arose from country to country as the process unfolded. These differences can be traced to the peculiarities of each country with respect to resource endowment, productive structure, and relationships with the outside world and political factors, as they presented themselves during the second half of the nineteenth century.

The variations were not large enough to outweigh the common denomi-
nators which can be observed among the five countries in many facets
of their economic experience, but proved to be of sufficient import to
affect: (a) the degree of development achieved by the export
economy, (b) the timing of the establishment and growth of the new
productive activities, and (c) the way in which the attendant problems
were solved.

Perhaps the most striking difference to be observed is that of the
lower degree of development attained by the new export economy in
Nicaragua and Honduras, as compared with Costa Rica, El Salvador
and Guatemala. Apparently the physical resources required for the
cultivation of coffee--such as land and water--were not as extensive
in size or as good in quality in the former two, as they were in the
latter three countries. There were other factors, however, which were
probably of greater importance.

Owing in part to the peculiar conditions of internal politics, as
they related to the question of foreign intervention, a long period of
conservative rule was inaugurated in Nicaragua upon the termination
of the war of 1856-57 with a Central American victory.[18] The
processes leading toward economic liberalism were thus submerged for
more than three decades. When they emerged, in the early 1890's,
new external and internal realities were at work, which prevented the
carrying out of significant reforms of the agrarian structure, the credit
system and so forth, as had been done elsewhere in Central America.
Uppermost among these realities seems to have been the recurrence of
the old problem of interoceanic communication, backed now by the
undisputed power of the United States in the area, and followed by
the actual occupation of the Nicaraguan territory between the early
1910's and the early 1930's.

All of these factors must have contributed decisively to the
limitations experienced by this country during the first stage of its
economic growth. In fact, it was not until after World War II that
Nicaragua was able to raise its agricultural export economy to a level
comparable with those of Costa Rica, El Salvador, and Guatemala.
But by now there was a set of circumstances, regarding the operations
of government and of the commodity and financial markets of the
world, wholly different from those prevailing in the latter part of the
nineteenth century.[19]

The continuing emphasis on an orientation of the economy toward the mining industry limited the growth of the Honduran agricultural export economy after the war of 1856-57. Having been the main mining center of the Spanish crown in Central America, Honduras could not escape the powerful influence exerted in this direction by the California gold rush, and the many people who went to and from the West Coast via the Central American Isthmus.[20] The internal political and administrative fragmentation inherited from colonial times and the high degree of vulnerability to political events in Guatemala and El Salvador[21] further handicapped the establishment of permanent foundations for a commercial economy of national scope, based upon the development of renewable resources.

The repercussions of the Guatemalan liberal reform movement added to political instability in Honduras after 1870. With the subsequent triumph of liberalism in this country, the road was paved for creating an export economy of its own, as in much of the rest of Central America. By this time, however, foreign interests had succeeded in gaining a firm foothold in the north coast and in getting well underway the development of the banana industry, which soon became the dominating activity.

Other agricultural exports such as coffee, were just beginning to grow. The local interests in these activities did not have as yet a comparable degree of control over the required land resources, were not backed by the necessary financial means, could not compete advantageously for the available manpower and were soon crushed by the much superior means which the banana industry had at its disposal in all of these aspects. Not uncharacteristically, it was not long before the political system became almost entirely subservient to the interests of this industry, a relationship which was to last well into the present century. The liberal reforms were never really consumated, and to this day Honduras still lacks a truly national commercial export economy of its own.

The experiences of Costa Rica, El Salvador and Guatemala also varied from country to country. The differences seem to have been related to: (a) the achievement of a reasonable measure of internal order at different points in time and (b) the ways in which the population was finally organized in the new productive structures, and the corresponding differences that emerged in the relationships between man and resources.

In Costa Rica, for example, internal order had been consolidated at an early date and there were no large reserves of a quasi-slave manpower. Thus, it was possible in this country to apply the full energies of a free labor force and the potentialities of a tradition of hard work to the development of the coffee industry well before it could even be started in the rest of the region. Unlike the colonists of Guatemala, the settlers of Costa Rica never had a large indian population on which they could draw for the establishment of "haciendas" and other forms of economic organization based upon relationships of servitude. Throughout the colonial period and well into the nineteenth century, they lived in a state of chronic poverty and lack of economic opportunity in a subsistence economy based largely on small land holdings. It was out of this experience that there emerged in Costa Rica the strong sentiment of equality among the population that constituted the background against which the export economy was to develop and that, in spite of subsequent changes, still characterizes the operations of its political and economic systems.

El Salvador, on the other hand, was the last of the Central American countries to develop an export economy based upon the coffee industry. It was not until the 1890's that coffee production started to grow rapidly in this country. This late start was directly related to the limitations arising out of the existing land tenure system, with its widespread elements of communal property (ejidos). The change to a system of private ownership did not begin in earnest until the 1880's when the liberal agrarian reform was carried out. Though belated, this reform was so wide in scope that it made it possible to carry the growth of the plantation economy and the development of the coffee industry to their most advanced stages in all of Central America.

The case of Guatemala depicts a more complex situation. As the capital of the Capitanía General, this province had received the heaviest influx of Spanish settlers during the colonial period and its economy had reached higher levels of development than the rest of the region as regards agriculture, local manufactures, trade and government. Side by side there persisted a strong indian culture, with its own economy and institutions, deeply rooted to their own land. This basic factor did not prevent the liberal movement from pushing vigorously the interests of the new export system, from easing the tight grip of the Church upon income and resources, and from making large blocks of manpower available to coffee cultivation and harvesting. But it was never possible to drive a lasting wedge between the indian peasant and his land. In addition to this, the resilience of some of the economic heritage of colonial rule led, throughout the following decades, to the maintenance of a system which is much more diverse in Guatemala than in any of the other Central American countries.

Significance of these Experiences for Multinational Economic Integration

An adequate explanation of these and other differences among the Central American countries still awaits the results of much fuller investigations into their economic history. Nevertheless, it is necessary to have a broad grasp of the issues involved, in order to understand some of the present problems, particularly those of the multinational economic integration of the region. For these countries come to such a venture not only with the elements that are common and that tend to unite them, but also with those that, being peculiarly the lot of each, tend to differentiate them as regards their problems, their interests, their weaknesses, and their strengths. As will be seen later, it is in the appropriate articulation of their differential economic outcomes into the going concern of a common market that the answers lie to some of the crucial questions regarding the viability of a Central American economy.

The search for these answers must start from the fact that the liberal reforms of the nineteenth century were substantially realized only in Costa Rica, where they worked against a background of equality that made possible the spread of basic education and the establishment of a stable civil government. In the remaining countries the reforms undoubtedly contributed, in varying degrees, to the development of the export economy, but they were largely frustrated in their attempts to improve the educational system and political administration. Their history, therefore, has been characterized by chronic governmental instability, accompanied by frequent military uprisings. The grafting of the export economy on the social structure inherited from colonial times has, in fact, contributed to the concentration of political power in small sectors of the population.

Similarly, the existence of powerful concentrations of means of investment in El Salvador and Nicaragua as against their relative dispersion in the other three countries; the more acute shortage of entrepreneurial resources in Nicaragua and Honduras, and the latter's lack of the more elementary works of an economic infrastructure, are all factors to be reckoned with in any attempt to tackle the important

question of balance among countries.[22] Finally, the latent popular
ferments in Guatemala and El Salvador, that are traceable to the land
tenure and farm labor arrangements of the export economy under
conditions of high rates of population growth, are likely to influence
political and economic development in these countries in ways that
cannot fail to condition the direction and progress of economic integration. The same is true as regards: (a) the continuing political
vacuum in Honduras, resulting from the absence of a national export
economy and from the weakening of the traditional relationship
between the political system and the foreign-owned export industry;
(b) the stresses and strains that are likely to lead to the change of the
political structure with which Nicaragua has developed her agricultural export economy in recent decades, and (c) the growing
incompatibilities between an ambitious social welfare system and a no
longer growing traditional economy in Costa Rica.

Footnotes to Chapter 2

1. In 1825 total Central American exports stood at 8.2 million
pesos, of which 7.0 million were contributed by cochineal
(2.5 million), indigo (2.0 million), cacao (1.5 million) and gold and
silver (1.0 million). See Solórzano Fernández, op. cit.,
pp. 244-245.

2. For incidences of this search see Carmen S. de Malavassi and
Belén André S., El Café en la Historia de Costa Rica (San José,
Costa Rica: University of Costa Rica, 1958), pp. 4-11,
/mimeographed/. Also, Soley Güell, op. cit., Vol. I and Facio,
op. cit.

3. Facio, op. cit., pp. 28-30.

4. Solórzano Fernández, op. cit., pp. 266-268.

5. Ibid., pp. 287-292; Torres, op. cit., pp. 179-183.

6. See Chapter 3 below.

7. Antonio Di Fulvio, El Café en el Mundo (Rome, Italy:
International Institute of Agriculture, 1947), p. 183; Monterrey,
op. cit., p. 514; Malavassi & André, op. cit., pp. 16-17; Torres,
op. cit., p. 190; Solórzano Fernández, op. cit., pp. 263-266.

8. Di Fulvio, op. cit., p. 153.

9. Stacy May & Galo Plaza, La United Fruit Company en América Latina (Mexico City: National Planning Association, 1959), pp. 8-14, 20-21.

10. See Di Fulvio, op. cit., pp. 114-115.

11. For figures covering the period 1880-1924 see Johannes Toppel, Die Banane Chemisch (Berlin: Technischer Verlag der Bodenbinder, 1935); and W. Bitter, Die Wirtschaftliche Eraberung Mittelamerikas durch die Bananen, Trustorganisation und imperialistische Bedeutung der United Fruit Company (Hamburg: G. Westernman, 1921); for the period 1925-29 see national official statistics.

12. May & Plaza, op. cit.; Oscar de León Aragón, Los Contratos de la United Fruit Company y las Compañías Muelleras de Guatemala (Guatemala: Editorial del Ministerio de Educación Pública, 1950) y Contratos celebrados entre el Gobierno de Honduras, la Cuyamel Fruit Company y la Tela Railroad Company (Tegucigalpa, Central Bank's Library), /Mimeographed7.

13. Solórzano Fernández, op. cit., pp. 282-283; Soley Güell, op. cit., Vol. I. pp. 288-295.

14. John Parke Young, Central American Currency & Finance (Princeton: Princeton University Press, 1925).

15. For a brief review of the foreign borrowing experience of Central America, see: United Nations, Foreign Capital in Latin America (New York, 1955), pp. 75, 93, 96, 105 and 120.

16. See, Soley Güell, op. cit., Vol. I, pp. 290-292.

17. See Naciones Unidas, La politica tributaria y el desarrollo económico en Centroamérica (Sales No. 1957, II. G.9), Chapter VIII.

18. Formally, the North American filibuster invasion was arranged by the liberal groups centered in the city of León. See Luis Alberto Cabrales, Historia de Nicaragua (Managua, 1951), p. 64.

19. For a detailed account of these recent processes see United Nations, Economic Commission for Latin America, Análisis y Proyecciones del Desarrollo Económico. IX. El Desarrollo Económico de Nicaragua (E/CN.12/742), Mexico, 1965, /mimeographed/.

20. Ralph J. Roberts & Earl M. Irving, Mineral Deposits of Central America, Department of the Interior, Geological Survey Bulletin 1034, (Washington, D. C., 1957), pp. 36-38. See also William V. Wells, Explorations & Adventures in Honduras (New York: Harper & Brothers, 1857).

21. See, for example, William S. Stokes, Honduras: An area study in government (Madison: The University of Wisconsin Press, 1950), pp. 40-41).

22. See Chapter 13 below.

CHAPTER 3

LIMITED CHANGE AND PERSISTENCE OF TRADITIONAL ACTIVITIES

The Contrasting Patterns of the Dual Economy

Far reaching though it was in significance, the development of the export economy did not make for universal change in the Central American systems, so as to give rise, with the passage of time, to totally new social and economic structures in the region. On the contrary, the process of transformation was limited only to certain segments, namely, export production, import trade and the related transport facilities, banking services, and communications with the rest of the world.

Large portions of the original systems remained intact. Agricultural production for the domestic markets continued to be carried out largely on a subsistence basis; even now there remain important elements of self-sufficiency in the production of staple foods. Manufacturing remained at the handicraft or cottage industry stage. Internal transport and communication facilities were built in the urban zones and in coffee and banana plantations, but little was done in other areas to facilitate the process of national integration. In a very real sense, the people living in the main cities and seaports are still much closer to the world centers of industry and trade than they are to the farther corners of their own territories.

The traditional sectors of the economy have remained unchanged in themselves. Not so in their relationships with the rest of the system. Obviously such relationships had to change in the presence of other rapidly growing economic sectors. This differential behavior has been an important source of the developmental stresses and strains that have been experienced by the Central American economies.

The limited extent of the changes brought about by the first
upsurge of economic development influenced also the organizational
structures within which the new activities flourished. Coexisting with
the old, they took on some of their characteristics. For example, the
coffee plantations brought about a certain degree of monetization in
the labor market, but the labor force continued to be organized to
a large extent on the same basis of serf-lord relationships that
characterized the old "hacienda." Although the ruling class changed,
the government expanded, and the liberal reforms were adopted, strong
paternalistic elements continued to permeate the exercise of political
power. By their very nature, these characteristics tended to confine
the process of growth and to diminish the effective operation of new
forces that might have brought about an integral type of development.

Psychological and Ideological Constraints on the Propagation of Growth

In addition to the external factors mentioned in the previous
chapter, these phenomena of limited change and persistence of traditional activities grew out of the interaction of two sets of factors:
First, the psychological and ideological forces underlying the outward
process of growth; second, the physical and economic characteristics
of this process. It was within the constraints established by these
factors that production of agricultural export commodities arose as the
main avenue for the achievement of economic growth. And it was
with reference to this peculiar orientation that changes were effected
in the nature and workings of property, citizenship and political
power.

Psychologically and ideologically, nineteenth century Central
America followed a one-sided orientation, wherein agricultural
production for export was what really counted, so that change in the
existing system had to be effected only to the extent required for the
achievement of this objective. In the prevailing scheme of things,
and according to the principle of international specialization, import
trade, not industrialization, provided the way to satisfy the growing
demand for manufactured goods.

These attitudes were, of course, conditioned by the fact that the
stimulus to economic growth came to Central America from the outside,
in the form of larger, more remunerative markets for the products of
their efforts and resources. But, at the same time, the external source

of this stimulus imposed limitations of its own on the process of growth. For it meant that the new opportunities open to Central America were not of its making and were not subject to its control. The countries of the area had to adjust their productive structures to the conditions of the world market, taking them almost wholly as given. In so doing, their actions were conditioned by the demand and supply structures of the more developed countries, as well as by the then existing differentials in the natural and technological resource endowments of center and periphery.

The identification of these constraining elements gives only a partial explanation of the phenomenon of limited change in the first stage of Central American economic growth. The rest of the story must be sought in the way the Central American countries reacted to them; that is to say, in the manner in which they used the possibilities inherent in the situation to promote the expansion of productive activity and to distribute the fruits so obtained among the various segments of the population. For this purpose, it is necessary to focus the inquiry, however briefly, on the changes which were effected in land tenure and the system of property relationships which grew out of the particular policies pursued in the process.

Land Policy

Two basic factors provided the frame of reference within which land policy came to be formulated in the Central American countries during the nineteenth century. First, this policy had to act upon an established system of land tenure relationships typified by the old "hacienda" and the small, subsistence farming unit. This was quite different from the situation in the United States, for example, where there were vast, practically empty expanses of uncultivated land that was not under private ownership. Second, land policy had to operate within fairly narrow geographic limits. Endemic disease prevailing over relatively large areas and the absence of large immigration movements effectively checked the possibilities of any significant process of colonization.

Within this frame of reference, the land problem consisted in the distribution of public (state, municipal) lands, incorporation of the landed property of the Church and of the communal properties ("ejidos") adjoining the towns into the private sector, and adjustment of the "hacienda" to the requirements of new resource uses. Public lands came into private hands through a policy of grants or sales at nominal prices, while Church lands were secularized upon the triumph of liberalism. Communal properties were broken in the wake of modern civil legislation and by means of special laws. Adjustments in the "hacienda" system were effected with the aid of government incentives designed to promote production of agricultural export commodities. The policy of grants was adopted, for example, in Costa Rica, and gave rise later to strong criticism characterizing it as a large scale squandering of public property.[1] The Guatemalan liberal agrarian reform of the 1870's relied on the secularization of church properties and, to a much larger extent, on the massive distribution of public lands.[2] Finally, the conversion of communal lands ("ejidos") into private property was the main process in El Salvador.[3]

Land policy was fundamentally concerned with the creation of a system of property relationships based upon private ownership and individual operation, though occasionally it was associated with other objectives. Costa Rica and Guatemala, for example, sought to attract immigrants for settlement and colonization, by means of grants and equal treatment to both nationals and foreigners. At times land sales were intended to alleviate the chronic fiscal problems of the governments, as in Costa Rica and El Salvador.[4] But nowhere in Central America did public policy discriminate between those who could and those who could not own land, nor did it impose limitations on the size and use of holdings. This was in line with the principles of liberalism, which could operate without restrictions in this case, given the abundance of the supply of land in relation to its demand in the region.

Economic Determinants of Land Concentration

The situation changed radically when access to the world markets for agricultural commodities opened up new resource-use opportunities. It was in the process of realizing these opportunities that the distribution of land and its organization into a productive process became critical. Coffee production, for example, implied technical requirements far more exacting than those of any of the crops which the farm operator of the day was used to growing. At the same time, it confronted farmers with previously unknown financial needs for both investment and current expenditures and made it indispensable to operate in a more complex commercial environment involving a series of industrial, banking and shipping functions, all of them new to the workings of the economic system.

In these circumstances, property in land became economically meaningful only when coupled with technical and commercial ability as well as with financial opportunity.[5] These complementary factors were scarce and unevenly distributed. That is why, in spite of its relative abundance, land came to be concentrated in the hands of those who could successfully utilize it in the production of export commodities. Thus, what land policy did not do in the way of discriminating between those who could and those who could not own land, the market did through the unimpeded actions of differences in technical knowledge and differential access to financial and commercial processes and institutions.[6]

The resulting system of ownership was rapidly structured around the plantation as the central type of organization in the agricultural export sector. It gave rise to a large labor force and a relatively small number of land owners. Distinct groups arose among the latter, with respect to size of holdings and relative measure of economic power. It thus became possible to differentiate between those who confined themselves to the agricultural phases of coffee production, those who in addition engaged in processing and credit functions,and those who completed the process of vertical integration with shipping abroad.

Similar outcomes were observed in the development of the banana industry, although the processes which brought them about differed in some respects from those that occurred in coffee production. For one thing, the growth of this industry was based upon the opening of new lands that were not subject to the traditional system of land tenure. For another, the fact that production techniques were in the hands of those who at the same time controlled the transportation and marketing functions led to the almost total vertical integration of this industry, in which little opportunity was left for Central Americans to participate, except in the provision of labor. Finally, the generous land grants, provided under the long-term concession contracts described earlier, contributed further to the concentration of land in large holdings to a far greater degree than in the rest of the export sector.

The Structure of Property and the Political System

This system of limited participation in the structure of ownership, where there remained large segments of landless people, was also a system of limited citizenship. The liberal constitutions of the period provided for universal suffrage and eligibility to public office, subject only to minimum requirements of age and place of birth. But, for the bulk of the population, real access to the political system and ability to act effectively before the governments were severely limited by weaknesses derived from lack of land or control over other resources.

All this contributed to a high degree of concentration of political power, which came to be exercised increasingly on behalf of the emerging class of property owners--foreign corporations included --operating in the external trade sectors. For some time political power was shared with the traditional elite of merchants and "hacienda" owners. But the political influence of this class diminished with the loss of its economic basis, and its remnants were finally left only with the enjoyment of social status.

In the evolution of control over governmental action, as it took place in Central America, independence from the Spanish Crown eliminated whatever conditions there might have been for a gradual process of assertion of private rights. This contrasts with the experience in some European countries, particularly England, where "the right of private property in land emerged from the struggle of 450 years between the sovereign as landlord and his vassals as tenants, over the rental value of land."[7] A political vacuum was thus created in Central America, which was filled temporarily by the traditional merchants and "hacienda" owners and by the clergy. However, their tenure was shortlived, since their power was based on a stagnant type of productive activity. They were finally replaced by the rising coffee growers and banana producers, whose economic base was much stronger and more dynamic. The interesting fact to be noted here is that, given the particular distributive characteristics of this process, in filling up the political vacuum, public and private power became one and the same thing for most practical purposes.

Having adopted the instrumentality of constitutional, representa-tive democracy, it was necessary to make substantial adjustments in its utilization, so as to take account of the political realities just described. A perfect adjustment was of course impossible to achieve. This explains, at least in part, the almost chronic state of instability that has charac-terized political life in Central America since independence.

Economic Constraints on the Propagation of Growth

In the light of the foregoing analysis it is possible to identify the internal economic factors that made for limited change and the persistence of traditional activities, in addition to the psychological and ideological forces and the economic variables of a purely external nature that have been mentioned previously.

On the demand side, the possibilities of diversified economic development--of industrialization and growth of modern service activities--were effectively checked by the limited extent of the internal market. This was originally limited on account of the small size of the Central American population and the lack of a sizable immigration movement, and had been fragmented as a result of the disintegration of the federal republic. The new system of property relationships, with its relatively large numbers of propertyless people, further weakened the growth potential of the internal market. It gave rise to a distribution of wealth and income that, rather than compensating for the limitations of small numbers, tended to limit further the demand for domestic products.

The consumption patterns that emerged in the context of the new structure of wealth and income distribution may have exerted an additional depressive influence upon the level of wages and upon their share in the national product. The development of an agricultural export economy not only brought the Central American economies into contact with the international commodity markets. It also brought small segments of the Central American populations--the property owners, coffee growers, export and import traders--into contact with the culture and consumption patterns characteristic of society in the more advanced countries.

Close ties developed between them. The financial interests of the wealthier Central Americans were handled in the banking centers of the world; their children went to school in France, England, Germany and the United States; their families acquired the tastes and consumption habits prevailing in these countries.[8] And since the economic base upon which they operated was much less productive than that of the systems whose culture they borrowed, maintenance of such cultural islands in Central America was only possible on the basis of low wages and a highly skewed distribution of income; that is to say, on the basis of placing additional limitations upon the extent of the internal market. Obviously, the system of limited participation in the structure of

ownership and the bargaining situation in which wage earners found
themselves, were conducive to the development of precisely such
conditions.

On the supply side, the diversification of the economy was limited
by a shortage of capital funds and by the imperfect knowledge of
modern technology. Given the high concentration of wealth and
income in the region, one would expect that internal savings were
large, so as to make available funds for financing new ventures in
manufacturing or in public utilities, in addition to those reinvested in
the export sector. But in all likelihood the rate of saving was relatively
low, and certainly lower than in the industrial countries.[9] The reason
for this, as already noted, was the high level and pattern of consumption
induced among the high income groups by their contact with the more
advanced cultures of Europe and North America.

On the other hand, the governments of the period, reflecting the
interest of these same groups, were neither strong enough nor inclined
to use taxation as a source of finance for public investment. They
relied almost exclusively on revenue from import duties, which was
highly unstable and frequently insufficient to meet current expenditures. As mentioned earlier, the inflow of foreign loan funds did not
reach significant proportions; and in the end, the various governments
had to resort to direct investments of foreign companies for the
construction of the main railways, ports and communication services
in the region.

But foreign capital from this source was concentrated on infrastructural facilities for the development of agricultural exports and,
to a lesser extent, on electric power services for the main cities, where
it had an assured market and was guaranteed adequate returns on
investment through long-term concession contracts. Little if any went
into other productive activities, particularly manufacturing, because
the small domestic markets did not offer sufficient inducements to
foreign investors, considering the risks involved in relation to
alternative opportunities elsewhere. Thus, as recently as 1950,
United States direct investments in manufacturing amounted to less
than 5 million dollars (book value) for the region as a whole, as
compared with a total of nearly 250 million dollars in other sectors,
mainly agriculture and public utilities.[10]

If conditions were unfavorable for foreign entrepreneurs to establish new industries for the regional markets, they were even more so for local investors, who were not familiar with modern technology and were further handicapped by the lack of managerial talent and trained manpower. The acquisition of industrial techniques developed in the more advanced countries, and their adaptation to the Central American environment, would have been, at best, a slow and laborious process. But, until comparatively recent years, little or no effort was made to create the means conducive to that process, as government economic policy was centered almost exclusively on the promotion of commodity exports.

The upshot of what has been said above concerning internal demand and supply relationships is that, given the prevailing external conditions and the psychological and political forces that shaped the way in which the Central American countries went about the business of developing their agricultural exports, the phenomenon of limited change and persistence of traditional activities and institutions was quite in line with the realities of the day. The required economic conditions were lacking for a more pervasive process which, springing from the initial thrust provided by exports, would have proceeded with the development of a diversified system of industrial and service activities. In this context, therefore, the three-way relationships between limited participation in the structure of ownership, limited citizenship and concentration of political power, could and did function in what might be characterized as a circular fashion, ever reinforcing the very factors and processes that confined growth to a relatively small number of sectors of the economy.

Footnotes to Chapter 3

1. Soley Güell, op. cit., Vol. I, pp. 216-218.

2. Solórzano Fernández, op. cit., pp. 287-291.

3. Torres, op. cit., pp. 180-184.

4. Solórzano Fernández, op. cit., pp. 284-285; Soley Güell, op. cit., Vol. I, p. 219.

5. For an analysis of the nature and interrelationships of ability, opportunity and property, see J. R. Commons, Legal Foundations of Capitalism (Madison: The University of Wisconsin Press, 1959), pp. 155-157.

6. Facio, Estudio sobre economía costarricense (San José, Costa Rica: Editorial Surco, 1942), p. 26; José Manuel Salazar, Tierras y Colonización en Costa Rica (Tesis de Grado, Universidad de Costa Rica, 1962), pp. 71-87; and Torres, op. cit., pp. 198-199.

7. Commons, op. cit., p. 200.

8. This phenomenon characterizes the general case in the developing nations, as was early pointed out by Raul Prebisch in: The Economic Development of Latin America and its Principal Problems (United Nations, 1950), pp. 5, 6, 37. Its effects on the propensity to save in developing countries were more fully analyzed by Ragnar Nurkse in: Problems of Capital Formation in Underdeveloped countries (Oxford: Basil Blackwell, 1953), Chapter III.

9. This may be more the general case of the developing nations, than a situation exclusively confined to Central America. See, for example, Nicholas Kaldor, "Problemas Económicos de Chile," El Trimestre Económico (Mexico City: Fondo de Cultura Económica), Vol. XXVI (2) No. 102, pp. 170-221.

10. See United Nations, Foreign Capital in Latin America, op. cit., Appendix Table XV; and United States Department of Commerce, U. S. Investments in the Latin American Economy (Washington, D. C.: U. S. Government Printing Office, 1957), Table 123.

CHAPTER **4** STRUCTURAL IMBALANCES
IN THE OUTWARD PROCESS
OF ECONOMIC GROWTH

The expansion of agricultural exports brought about a substantial
process of economic growth in Central America. But it also confronted
the countries of the region with new problems, that can be traced
largely to the risks and difficulties inherent in the development and
functioning of a modern commercial economy. Some of them, however,
are related to the way in which the Central American countries
organized themselves, particularly in the area of property structures and
relationships, and to the scope and nature of the changes in resource
use that were induced by the considerable gains obtained in the
production of agricultural export commodities.

The more pressing and visible problems have been associated with
the recurrent fluctuations in the demand for Central American products
arising from economic crisis in the industrial countries. But the less
obvious problems of an imbalanced resource use structure have perhaps
been of even greater significance for the long-run growth of the
regional economy.

The Impact of Export Production upon the Traditional Pattern of Resource Use

Before the development of the coffee industry, the Central
American people, living as they were in accordance with rather
elementary standards, were able to satisfy most of their needs with
domestic goods and services. They produced their own food staples--
corn and beans--, their own meat, sugar, wheat, liquor and tobacco,

as well as cotton, from which they wove the rougher cloths that met most of the population's requirements. Imports were, therefore, confined almost solely to fine textiles, hats,and a few other luxury items.[1]

With the advent of coffee production, important changes took place in resource use and in the level and structure of demand, which radically changed this situation. Competition for the same supplies of land and labor became keener. At the same time, the newly es- tablished connections with the international commercial economies permitted the introduction of imports which not infrequently were highly competitive with Central American production.

Two cases may be distinguished. Firstly, in those areas where the forces of competition were stronger, operating at the same time in the land and labor markets, as well as in the local versus imported products markets, the traditional lines of activity quickly disappeared, giving way to ever larger landscapes of the familiar dark green coffee plan- tations. It was in this way that wheat and cotton made their exit from the Central American economies, and that wheat flour and cotton textiles,from the newly developed North American plains,and from the British mills,made their entry into the consumption patterns of the Central American population.[2]

Secondly, in those areas where the above mentioned competitive forces were weaker, operating mainly in the labor market, the traditional lines of activity remained important contributors to the national product. This was the case of corn, beans,and sugar cane whose cultivation was displaced to the poorer soils, farther away from the existing means of transportation and population centers. The production of these crops remained technologically stagnant, because the small extent of the market and their peculiar input coefficients precluded the absortion of large amounts of labor per unit of output, as in the coffee and banana plantations. Nearly a century would have to elapse before technological advances--such as hybrids, pesticides and chemical fertilizers--could make any headway i n improving the production of food staples in the region.

A new structure of resource use thus emerged in the Central American countries as a result of the interplay of economic forces, with the producers of coffee and bananas out ahead in the race for manpower and physical resources, with some traditional lines of activity being pushed to poorer lands and others quickly disappearing from the scene. The main components of the resulting system were the export sector and its allied trading, transportation, communications, and financial activities, on the monetary side of the economy, and the food sector, on the mainly subsistence side.

The export sector performed the commanding role in the new system, with the others, save that of food production, being tied thereto by a simple, one-way relationship of direct dependence. The relative independence of the food sector was rooted essentially in its being a non-monetized subsistence type of operation. This one-sided orientation of the economy, wherein general development depends on the growth of one sector and not on the mutually reinforcing behavior of its various components, constitutes one of the fundamental facts in the economic history of the Central American countries.

Several economic and technological relationships underlay the problems encountered in the operation of this new system. The most important of these was the lack of correspondence between the composition of the resource endowment and the nature of the factor demands of the new export lines of production. Whereas the supply of labor was small, relative to that of land, manpower requirements for coffee and banana production were large, relative to those of other factors. In fact, labor was the largest component of the inputs for both the establishment and the operation of the plantations and their allied infrastructural facilities.

In these circumstances the tapping and full utilization of the relatively short supply of labor acquired overriding importance. At the same time, the resources had to be allocated in such a way as to provide for the growth of exports and for the continued fulfillment of the food needs of the population. The difficulties and relative success achieved in attempting to solve these two problems can be understood only with reference to the ways in which Central Americans organized themselves to take advantage of the new opportunities offered by the external markets.

The Food and Export Sectors: Their Differentiation and Interrelationships

The main features of the new organization grew out of the polarization of economic activity into two sectors: Production for export and food production for the home market. The export sector was composed mainly of the commercial banana and coffee plantations, though family-sized farms were not infrequent in coffee production, particularly in Costa Rica, as the remnants of the pre-existing system of land distribution. Export mining was also carried out by commercial firms, mostly foreign-owned, but it was of relatively minor importance, with the possible exception of Nicaragua, where commercial agriculture for export did not fully develop until recent decades. The typical production unit in the food sector, on the other hand, was much smaller and often barely sufficient to meet the needs of the family that worked in it. There was no relationship between the export and the food sectors in the product markets, since one served an international, fully monetized market and the other served primarily the subsistence needs of rural families and only secondarily the domestic, non-farm population. The export sector, however, depended on the food sector for a substantial proportion of its labor supply.

The development of export production as a separate sector established specific conditions for the solution of the labor problem. Money wages were the main inducement for the transfer of rural workers to the plantations, along with a variety of legal devices designed to cut off the peasant population from free access to land, such as the creation of large property units.[3] But these were insufficient, and the governments often resorted to more direct, coercive means in an effort to meet the labor requirements of the rapidly growing export sector.[4]

Wage payments, as distinguished from imputed labor returns, gave rise to an important monetary cost, thus tying the volume of production directly to the ups and downs of an uncertain and far removed market. Moreover, they tended to make the labor supply dependent on the reservation price of labor in terms of money. As suggested before, money wages had to be fixed at relatively low levels in order to make it possible for a given segment of the population to enjoy the consumption patterns of more advanced societies, though living out of a much less productive system.

Consequently, not enough labor was forthcoming at the going wages, and in some countries, notably Guatemala and Nicaragua, it became necessary to enact special legislation and to use the administrative apparatus of the government in order to force people to work in the plantations.[5]

This system was relatively successful in satisfying the labor requirements of plantations. One wonders, however, whether better

results could not have been achieved by relying more on the willing
participation of the people and on cooperative arrangements that are
rooted in a strong social institution, such as the family unit. To some
extent, this is the Costa Rican experience, where family-sized farms
constitute a much larger component of the coffee industry. But, even
in this country, it was always difficult to arrive at a satisfactory
solution to the problem of fulfilling the seasonal labor requirements.

One can readily see the difficulties involved in operating a
system of money wages in a rural economy with a poorly developed
financial system, as well as those that must emerge out of the application of coercive devices in a liberal society which has officially
declared itself against slavery. But it is also evident that the
adoption of an alternative system presupposed a different structure of
property ownership, as well as a vigorous public policy for the
dissemination of technical knowledge and the equalization of financial
and credit opportunities.

Under the impact of the rapidly growing export activities, the
labor supply for the food sector, in a very real sense, consisted of the
residual left by the monetized segment of agriculture. Large amounts
of labor were taken away from food production and devoted to export
crops on a permanent basis. Moreover, the food sector served as
a reservoir of labor for the fulfillment of the seasonal demand during
the harvesting periods. Thus labor shortages began to appear also in
the food sector, particularly in the old "haciendas," whose owners
could not pay the same wages as the plantations. Some of them,
however, were able to stem the outflow of labor by offering their
workers new incentives through the system of the "colonato". By means
of this arrangement the "haciendas" were divided into several plots,
each worked by the "colono" and his family on a share-cropping basis.
As the author was able to ascertain in personal interviews with
landowners in El Salvador, this form of land tenure still prevails in
some areas of that country.

The Paradox of Scarcity and Underutilization of Labor

The coffee harvest required large numbers of people for three to
four months of the year. From a narrow and purely commercial point
of view, it did not matter very much what these people did during the
rest of the year. In fact, many of them did nothing, while others
devoted their efforts to raising their own food staples. But even these

spent part their time in idleness. The extraordinarily wasteful phenomenon of the "tiempo muerto," so well known in the sugar economies of the Caribbean islands, thus became a permanent characteristic of life in Central America, as well.[6] It is difficult to conceive a more paradoxical situation in an economy where labor was scarce and there was a paramount need to utilize it fully.

The labor employed on a permanent basis in the plantations was also underutilized. The single-minded pursuit of profit from the cash crops resulted in a high degree of specialization within these farms. Given the changing nature of labor requirements throughout the year, the more specialized was the plantation, the higher was its degree of underutilization of available manpower. The coffee-sugar pattern of production offered a partial solution to this problem, particularly in certain areas of Costa Rica, but it did not become a generalized practice in the region as a whole.

A similar situation developed in the food producing farms, although for other reasons. In many instances labor was underutilized for lack of enough land to absorb it in the particular uses to which it was put. Other important limitations were the lack of capital equipment, even such elementary tools as animal power and the wooden plow, as well as those imposed by the one-crop-a-year pattern typical of the dry farming system.

Chronic Deficiencies in the Food Sector

The development of export and food crops in two distinct sectors conditioned the relative success of the Central American economies in achieving the twin objectives of maintaining high levels of foreign exchange earnings while fulfilling the basic internal needs of the population. Not long after the establishment of coffee production, a precarious equilibrium emerged between the food producing sectors and the rest of the system. Shortages of the main food staples began to appear in the area as early as the 1850's and, by the turn of the century, they had become a chronic phenomenon.[7]

Given the rudimentary technologies employed in food production, these shortages were due to some extent to crop failures arising from weather fluctuations, plagues and plant disease. But their increasing manifestations as a permanent feature of the Central American economies suggest that, in the face of a growing population, the food producing sector was left with an insufficient amount of resources to maintain a reasonable degree of self-sufficiency.[8] This can be explained largely by the fact that the internal markets were highly fragmented, thus preventing the price system from redressing the balance of resources in favor of food production. In the absence of tariff protection or other governmental measures for the promotion of local production, food shortages were met increasingly with imports from abroad.

These liberal policies tended to perpetuate the isolation of the food sector from the money economy, and to favor the production of export crops. For, in the absence of radical changes in the productivity of the system, the monetization of the food sector would have raised the wages paid by the coffee plantations, in relation to the level of export prices in the international markets, with the corresponding deterioration in profit margins. In addition, payment of relatively high prices for food staples would have provided farm workers with an alternative source of cash, thereby making it more costly to provide the plantations with their larger labor requirements during the harvest. As it happened, the food sector did not become monetized, the farm workers in the export plantations raised their own food, profit margins remained high, and the size of the market for food stayed small, relative to total output and total subsistence needs.

Under these conditions there was no incentive to build an agricultural infrastructure--e.g., irrigation works--to create external economies and to reduce the cost of food, so as to make possible a sizable increase in the output of export crops, as well as in the level and stability of food production. The construction of such an infrastructure would have resulted in a significant increase in the productivity of the system, stimulating the shift of resources into the export sector and making it possible to fulfill the food needs of the population at lower prices. But, as already noted, the institutional framework that evolved in Central America was not conducive to these ends, since it did little or nothing to promote the integration of the internal market and the willing participation of the people in public works programs, as part of a process leading to the full utilization of available labor resources.

Footnotes to Chapter 4

1. Soley Güell, op. cit., Vol. I, pp. 96-201, and Solórzano Fernández, op. cit., pp. 245-246.

2. Soley Güell, op. cit., Vol. II, pp. 27-28, and Solórzano Fernández, op. cit., p. 246.

3. For an analysis of this type of process, see Eric R. Wolf and Sydney W. Mintz, "Haciendas and Plantations in Middle America and the Antilles," Social and Economic Studies (Jamaica: University College of the West Indies, Institute of Social and Economic Research), pp. 381-412.

4. Sanford A. Mosk, "The Coffee Economy of Guatemala, 1850-1918; Development and Signs of Instability," Inter-American Economic Affairs, Vol. 9, No. 3 (Winter 1955), pp. 6-20.

5. Di Fulvio, op. cit., p. 158; "Ley sobre agricultura y trabajadores," Boletin Judicial, (Managua, 1920-43), and Solórzano Fernández, op. cit., pp. 313-314.

6. See, for example, Ramiro Guerra y Sánchez, Sugar & Society in the Caribbean (New Haven: Yale University Press, 1964).

7. Monterrey, op. cit., pp. 354, 365-366, 375; Soley Güell, op. cit., Vol. I, p. 337, Vol. II, pp. 27, 28, 62, 68, and Sanford A. Mosk, op. cit., pp. 6-20.

8. For an account of this process in Costa Rica, see Rodrigo Facio, La Moneda y la Banca Central en Costa Rica (Mexico City: Fondo de Cultura Económica, 1947), pp. 148-161.

CHAPTER **5** THE EXPORT ECONOMY
UNDER PERMANENT
INSTABILITY

In examining the problems faced by the Central American
economies as they developed, the analysis has centered so far on
their internal organization and on imbalances on the supply side.
The present chapter deals with problems arising out of the fluctuations
and long-term trends of external demand.

The general nature of these problems has been elucidated and is
well known.[1] The purpose here is to study their concrete expressions
in Central America, thus completing the picture of the development
of the region's export economy. It is necessary that this be done,
since the behavior of external demand helps to explain how the first
stage of economic development came to an end in these countries.

The Problems of Bimetallism in the Nineteenth Century

Between 1850 and the early 1900's, when the export economy was
established and achieved its highest rate of growth, the main source
of external disequilibrium were the fluctuations in the relative prices
of gold and silver. Inherited from Spain, the bimetallic monetary
system prevailed in the five countries throughout the nineteenth
century. The gold or the gold exchange standard, which was destined
to live a precarious existence in Central America, was not adopted
until 1900 in Costa Rica, 1912 in Nicaragua, 1918 in Honduras,
1920 in El Salvador and 1924 in Guatemala.

A shortage of silver developed during the 1850's, when gold was
relatively plentiful as a result of the discovery of new deposits in

California. But the really critical period was 1873-1916, when the price of silver decreased greatly and gold became relatively scarce. This resulted from the exhaustion of the new gold deposits, the widespread adoption of the gold standard among the more advanced countries, with their corresponding elimination of silver money, the discovery of new silver deposits, and the invention of higher yielding methods for processing this mineral. In addition, some silver came to Central America from Peru and Chile, when it was pushed out by the adoption of paper money in these countries during the war of 1879-85.[2]

The continuous rise in the price of gold in terms of silver acted as an obstacle to the adequate organization and general development of Central American economies precisely at the time when their export sectors were flourishing. The fact that imported merchandise had to be paid for in gold and then sold internally for silver of an uncertain and decreasing value introduced strong speculative elements in the system, pushed domestic prices upward, and generally influenced the operations and practices of the commercial sector. This same factor was unfavorable to investment in productive enterprises for the internal market, with their high import requirements, and contributed to make investment in export activities and in speculative ventures relatively more attractive.

The Modern Crises up to World War II

In Central America, as elsewhere, the typical crises of the export economy have been brought about by rapid falls of prices in the international markets. It was not until the great depression of the 1930's that reduced access to these markets began to emerge in the form of higher tariffs, internal consumption taxes, and import quotas, particularly in the Western European countries.

Excess output of export commodities in the producing countries and economic depressions in the importing countries were the main determinants. Occasional maladjustments between supply and demand and between the corresponding rates of growth of production and consumption started to occur around the turn of the century. Abnormally large coffee crops were harvested in 1897 and 1901 by the more important producing areas. This made for lower prices over the five-year period ending in 1902 and resulted in smaller earnings for all exporters, including the Central American countries.[3]

Export prices dropped again during the crisis after World War I (1920-22), and with greater intensity during the great depression of the 1930's. By this time, the occurrence of abundant coffee harvests in relation to world consumption had become a chronic phenomenon. Such was the case in 1927 and 1929, and again in 1933, 1934, and 1936.[4]

The two World Wars were critical periods for the export economies of Central America. The uncertainties which prevailed in the early stages of both conflicts, as regards the evolution of foreign trade, led to runs on the exchange markets and to faster liquidation of outstanding credit, thus straining the functioning of the financial system. It was difficult to assure steady and otherwise adequate supplies of imports and uninterrupted sales of exports in the traditional markets.

The volume and regularity of imports were inadequate both in 1914-19 and in 1940-45. The European continental market was closed to Central American exports during World War I. But shipping to London, which was the main market, was carried out under relatively normal conditions during the later years of that war.[5] In World War II all the European markets were closed to Central American exports. By then however, the United States had become the main market, and trade with this country was not interrupted though it was limited by the insufficiency of shipping facilities.

Economic Recovery During World War II and the Postwar Period

To some extent, the needs of the war effort and the difficulties encountered in satisfying import requirements of consumer goods stimulated economic activity in 1940-45. To be sure, the volume of traditional exports from Central America did not increase since the European market remained closed; shortages of shipping capacity continued, and access to the main United States market was subject to quotas and price controls. But some external stimuli arose in the form of new jobs and new commodity exports as the Canal operations expanded greatly in Panama: Large numbers of workers migrated to this country during this period, while the Canal Zone also absorbed substantial quantities of Central American fruits and vegetables. In addition, commercial production of hemp and natural rubber was started in some countries, e.g. Guatemala and Costa Rica, as part of an effort to make up for the loss to the Allies of their regular sources of supply in Southeast Asia. Consumer goods industries, such as textiles, vegetable oils, and flour milling began to be established as imported products became scarce.

However, these were weak and temporary stimuli. At no time were they strong enough, in comparison with the basic determinants of the existing system, to change the tide towards stagnation which had already set in. They disappeared soon after the war, when activities in the Canal Zone went back to their usual level and the regular sources of supply of imports returned to normal.

The first postwar decade was a period of almost unparalleled prosperity for most of the Central American countries, second only to the golden age of the traditional export economy between 1880 and 1900. Substantial amounts of international reserves, which had been accumulated during the war, supported the large expansion of imports required to satisfy deferred needs and new demands. Current foreign exchange earnings also increased rapidly, as a result of the favorable turn taken by the prices of Central American exports. The price of coffee, for example, more than trebled between 1945 and 1954.[6]

However, the level of output and the volume of traditional exports followed a different pattern during this period. Regional exports of bananas recovered quickly, from 15 to nearly 25 million stems yearly, once the shipping limitations disappeared; but they failed to reach the high levels of the early 1930's. This reflects the continuing diffi- culties faced by the industry in increasing yields, as well as the effects of new factors: Unrest in the ranks of its labor force; antitrust suits in the United States against the larger companies, and changes in the structure of demand.[7]

In the case of coffee, the supply response to higher prices lagged several years, owing to the technical characteristics of production. The productive capacity of existing plantations had deteriorated during the long period of depressed prices, when it was not profitable to utilize labor intensively as required by the best cultivation practices; this deficiency also reduced the capacity to absorb profitably modern inputs and postponed for some time the use of fertilizers, pesticides, and pump irrigation. Moreover, the development of new plantations required from three to five years, and not infrequently lands of lower quality had to be used for this purpose. All these factors precluded the achievement of large increases of output in the short run.

The wave of high prices made it possible to devote large areas to the production of cotton in El Salvador and Nicaragua and, to a lesser extent, in Guatemala and Honduras. Internal farm policy in the United States--one of the main exporters of the fiber--by virtue of which this country priced itself out of the international market for cotton,seems to have played an important, if unintended, role in the creation of this opportunity.

The new cotton areas had been utilized previously in an extensive manner as part of the traditional, largely subsistence agriculture, producing for the domestic market. Given the modern techniques of fertilization and insect control, the land could now be used very productively to take advantage of this export opportunity. It was the lack of these techniques that impeded the development of cotton production in Guatemala during the early 1860's.[8] A new economic activity was thus developed   which soon became one of the chief sources of foreign exchange earnings, provided for fuller utilization of the rural labor force and contributed to the transfer of modern technology to Central American agriculture.

The development of the cattle and the fishing industries as permanent additions to the export economy was also initiated during the first postwar decade. Modern slaughterhouses were constructed in Costa Rica and Nicaragua, making it possible to transform the traditional sales of live cattle to Peru and Curacao into exports of chilled meat, now oriented toward the United States and Puerto Rico. At the same time, extractive, processing,and shipping facilities were developed, which facilitated exports of highly valued products of the fishing industry.

In spite of the fairly intensive efforts that have gone into these activities, the results obtained to date and the prospects for the immediate future can only be characterized as modest. Much remains to be done in the cattle industry to increase productive capacity, to improve quality standards,and to consolidate market connections, while in the area of fisheries basic knowledge about the potential catch has yet to be acquired.

Postwar Fluctuations and Developments

Once more, prosperous times came to an end. Coffee prices fell sharply after 1955 as a result of pressures of greatly increased supplies in the international market. These were followed by similar, though less pronounced, declines in the price of cotton as a result of the United States re-entering the export market and of the growing competition of synthetic fibers of all kinds and origins. The crisis emerged in Central America in the familiar pattern of foreign exchange difficulties, fiscal insufficiencies, credit shortages, and unemployment.[9]

Developments in internal institutional arrangements that had taken place since 1950 made it possible to deal more effectively with this crisis that with earlier ones. Central banks, newly created in Guatemala (1946), Honduras (1950) and Costa Rica (1952), were in a better position to manage foreign exchange and internal credit policies, and to link them with the revenue and expenditure programs of the central governments. These institutions were also able to obtain financial aid from international credit agencies, which was to prove important in coping with the ensuing balance of payment difficulties. In addition, tariff policy was utilized increasingly to preserve the equilibrium of external transactions and as an instrument for promoting industrial growth.

The international institutions created after World War II have contributed in no small measure to the efficacy of these actions. They have provided short-term financing to reduce the impact of the deterioration in the foreign reserve position, as well as medium and long-term loans to cover the foreign exchange component of investment projects, especially in the fields of road construction, electric power, and agriculture. All five countries have engaged at various times in stand-by operations with the International Monetary Fund and have been assisted by the International Bank for Reconstruction and Development in financing development projects. These and other sources--the Eximbank, the Development Loan Fund, and more recently, the Agency for International Development and the Inter-American Development Bank--have contributed to maintain a sizable net inflow of capital funds in Central America since 1957, thus reversing the trend toward a net outflow of the early 1950's.[10]

With the entry into production of the new coffee plantations, the volume of exports started to grow rapidly around 1954, precisely when the crisis set in. It continued to increase throughout the more critical years--from 1957 to 1960 --as the prevailing price conditions spurred the widespread utilization of modern techniques in the coffee industry, as well as the rationalization of cost structures and organizational characteristics of cotton production. Thus the growth of the main components of agricultural exports was adjusted to lower prices, so that when the latter improved in 1961-63, the Central American economies recovered and then experienced a moderate expansion. [11]

The increased productivity of the external sector since 1955 prevented a substantial deterioration in the levels of income per head and permitted the importation of a larger volume of goods than would have been the case otherwise. But they were not enough to determine a satisfactory process of economic growth in the various countries, except perhaps in Nicaragua where, as previously mentioned, the agricultural export economy was at last fully developed during the postwar period. [12] In general, incomes per head were barely higher in 1963 than in 1958; several national governments were still plagued by fiscal and balance of payments difficulties. The net inflow of foreign capital had, in fact, only partially offset the loss of income resulting from the deterioration of the terms of trade between 1955 and 1962.

Footnotes to Chapter 5

1. See, for example, United Nations, Economic Commission for Latin America, Economic Survey of Latin America, 1949 (New York: 1951), pp. 3-85.

2. A detailed account of the protracted question of bimetallism may be found in Young, op. cit.

3. Di Fulvio, op. cit., pp. 153, 539.

4. Ibid., pp. 476-486, 537-545.

5. Soley Güell, op. cit., Vol. II, pp. 109-129.

6. Pan American Coffee Bureau, Coffee Statistics, No. 19 (New York: 1955), p. 70.

7. United Nations, Economic Commission for Latin America, "The International Banana Market - Its Evolution and Prospects," Economic Bulletin for Latin America, Vol. III, No. 2 (Santiago, Chile, October 1958), pp. 16-18, and Análisis y Proyecciones del Desarrollo Económico. XI. El Desarrollo Económico de Honduras (Mexico City, 1960), pp. 27-31.

8. See Solórzano Fernández, op. cit., p. 272.

9. United Nations, Economic Commission for Latin America, El sector externo y el desarrollo económico de Centroamérica, 1950-62 (Mexico City, 1964), pp. 1-6, /mimeographed/.

10. Ibid., p. 9.

11. United Nations, Economic Survey of Latin America, 1963 (New York, 1965), pp. 18-19.

12. See United Nations, Economic Commission for Latin America, El Desarrollo Económico de Nicaragua, op. cit.

6

END OF CENTRAL AMERICA'S FIRST STAGE OF ECONOMIC DEVELOPMENT

Long-term Trends Toward Stagnation

With the great depression of the early 1930's, the first stage of economic development came to an end in Central America. After roughly fifty years of steady growth (1850-1900), followed by three decades of increasing deficiencies, the agricultural export economy was no longer capable of performing as it did at the turn of the century. From 1930 onward, the system failed to provide sufficient employment opportunities for the increasing labor force. It did not allow for appreciable improvements in the levels of consumption of the population, nor did it furnish the means of investment required for maintaining high rates of economic growth.

This was the outcome of a trend toward stagnation reflecting the combined effects of several factors. First, the international markets for the region's exports gradually lost their initial dynamic conditions. Second, increasing difficulties on the supply side slowed down the growth of agricultural production for export. Third, the cumulative effects of recurrent business and fiscal crises made it more difficult to organize a substitute developmental impulse based on the domestic market.

The Evolution of Demand for Agricultural Exports

The demand for coffee and bananas grew at relatively satisfactory rates up to about 1930. World imports of coffee rose 2 per cent per annum between 1882 and 1930, while those of bananas increased several times in the same period. These rates of growth were not maintained thereafter. In the case of coffee, it decreased to 0.2 per cent per annum between 1930 and 1945, while the yearly increment of total banana imports barely reached 1 per cent during 1926-55.[1]

Various factors contributed to these trends. There was the natural tendency toward physical saturation of per capita consumption of coffee in markets of Western Europe and North America. There was also the effect of substitutes and of smaller fractions of the additions to personal income being spent by the consumer on this product. World per capita consumption of bananas has remained stagnant since the early 1930's, reflecting partially the effects of the depression and the disruption of trade during World War II. In addition, the very definite shift from fresh to processed fruits in the consumption patterns of the United States, which is the main traditional importer, has had an unfavorable impact upon the demand for bananas.[2]

The breakdown of multilateralism as the organizing principle of the international economy compounded the negative consequences of all of these factors. Measures designed to protect the national markets began to multiply since the 1930's, in the form of higher tariffs, import quotas, and preferential arrangements that were adopted by the United States and Western Europe.[3]

Thus, the traditional outlets for Central American exports ceased to provide the required stimulus for a continuing process of economic development. Moreover, with the introduction of soluble coffee since World War II, the Central American producers, along with those of other Latin American countries, have had to face the increasing competition of the lower grades of coffee from Africa in the American and European markets. The share of African coffee in the world market rose from less than 3 per cent in the early 1920's to 21 per cent in 1955.[4]

Numerous efforts have been made to put some order in the world coffee market since 1902. But, apart from the temporary marketing arrangements between the Latin American producers and the United States during World War II, none of them were successful until nearly all the producing countries of Latin America were able to sign an International Coffee Agreement in 1961.[5] The system of export quotas established under this agreement has made it possible to maintain some measure of stability in coffee prices, after their partial recovery from the low levels that prevailed between 1955 and 1960.

Diminished Impetus of Agricultural Production
for Export

A long-term trend toward stagnation of Central American agricultural production for export was superimposed upon the unfavorable
turn taken by demand conditions in the international markets. As a
result, the region's share of total world exports diminished substantially.
In the case of coffee, it was only 9.5 per cent in 1960, as compared
with 18.3 per cent in 1900,[6] while the share of banana exports
decreased from 54.1 to 36.7 per cent between 1924-28 and 1953-57.[7]

Coffee exports continued to increase after 1900, but at a much
slower rate. The best land for the production of this crop was already
under cultivation, and yields per acre did not improve, and even
deteriorated in times of crisis. In fact, during the Great Depression
and the war period, total regional exports of coffee were virtually
stagnant, having risen from an annual average of 121,000 metric tons
in 1925-29 to 136,000 in 1940-44.[8]

Banana production kept expanding for a longer period, but plant
diseases and losses in soil fertility started to develop around 1915. This
made it necessary to abandon many of the established plantations and
to shift production to new areas. Together with the depression in the
United States, these factors led not only to stagnation but to an actual
drop in production. After reaching a maximum in 1931, regional
exports of this product decreased continuously to volumes, which, at
the end of World War II, were approximately equal to those recorded
in 1910.

As noted earlier, other factors (labor conflicts, antitrust
proceedings in the United States, uncertainties arising from attempted
land reforms in one or two countries) have influenced the production
plans of the foreign fruit companies in Central America. As a result,
banana output during the postwar period has been kept at lower levels
than in the late 1920's. The production of coffee, on the other hand,
has been rising since the late 1950's; but much of this gain has been
wiped out by lower prices in the world market.

The Cumulative Effect of Periodic Crises

In the absence of adequate historical trade statistics, there is no
basis for arriving at firm conclusions concerning Central America's

long-run terms of trade. It is not implausible to suppose, however, that she shared, with other primary-producing areas, the effects of the long-run decline in the prices of primary products relative to those of manufactures that has been observed between the early 1870's and the immediate prewar years. Thus, according to calculations of the World Bank, the index measuring the terms of trade of primary products, for the world as a whole, showed a downward trend, from 112 in 1870 to 88 in 1929, and to 75 in 1938 (1913=100).[9]

But, quite apart from long-term influences, it can be said that the recurrent internal crises caused by the sharp fluctuations in the world market for agricultural products weakened Central America's capacity for achieving sustained economic growth. Moreover, the way in which these crisis were dealt with in the various countries may have contributed further to the stagnation that became apparent since the early 1930's.

The traditional pattern of crisis in Central America is all too familiar. Prices for exports decreased, resulting in smaller foreign exchange earnings and a depletion of reserves. Credit, imports and government revenues shrank, giving rise to unemployment and idle productive capacity. Barring other occurrences, an equilibrium of sorts was established at the lower level of economic activity warranted by the smaller income derived from exports.

In adjusting to the lower export incomes, the brunt of the burden was borne initially by the workers in the export sector, through loss of employment or lower wages. This tended to reduce the profit losses of the plantation owners and exporters, who, moreover, were able to obtain moratoria on interest and repayment of commercial debts. That a precarious equilibrium could be maintained for a while was due largely to the fact that the unemployed agricultural workers were partially reabsorbed by the subsistence sector of the economy, and those who remained on the plantations were able to grow their own minimum food requirements.

But, as the crisis continued, its depressive effects were soon felt in the urban centers, particularly in the construction and commercial activities. There was little that the governments could do to sustain the level of employment, hard pressed as they were by the contraction of revenue from foreign trade. However, they generally tried to maintain the pre-existing levels of expenditure; and in doing this they resorted to internal bank credit and the issue of paper money to finance their increasing deficit.

This, of course, further contributed to the deterioration of the balance-of-payments position, as the money supply expanded in the face of declining or stagnant foreign exchange earnings. With the consequent depletion of reserves, imports of consumer goods were cut down, giving rise to shortages in the domestic markets, price rises,and the depreciation of national currencies. One important consequence of this process was the virtual loss of access to the international financial markets, as most countries of the region were unable to service their foreign debts.[10] The only exception seems to have been El Salvador, where a policy of monetary stability and fiscal restraint was followed since the adoption of the gold standard in 1920.[11] But even this country was forced to adopt, during the depression of the 1930's, moratoria on bank debts and other unorthodox financial measures that were characterized at the time as symptoms of a "crisis in legality".[12]

The effects of the crisis and the derived obstacles to sustained growth usually persisted after the crisis itself was over and prices of exports had recovered their previous levels. This was particularly true of the fiscal system, as the governments continued to face deficit or were forced to devote a substantial fraction of their revenues to reduce the internal debt and to restore the monetary system to a healthier position. Such was the experience in Guatemala between 1897 and 1923 and in Nicaragua from 1893 to 1909, in the first case, and in Costa Rica during 1882-85, 1902-05, 1921-24, 1950-53 in the second.

The measures taken to cope with the crises succeeded at least in preventing the unemployment situation from getting out of hand. In this way, and through the financial assistance to the export sector, they contributed to the stability of the existing pattern of economic organization and the corresponding political power structure.

The distributive results of these actions should be noted. In effect, they must have amounted to large transfers of income from the rest of the economy to the export activities. These were effected largely through the reduction of the wage costs of coffee production and through the forced savings imposed on the population by the inflationary process. The devaluation of the national currencies also tended to favor the production of agricultural export, by making it more profitable (or less unprofitable during the crises) than production for the home markets.

It is precisely in the cumulative effect of such processes that another element of stagnation may have been added to the functioning of the Central American economies. Not only had they been initially organized in a way which prevented the propagation of growth from the export sector throughout the system, but also repeated experiences with external disequilibria had loaded the structure of relative prices more heavily in favor of the traditional export oriented activities. Correlatively, the diversification of productive enterprises for the internal market had become less and less attractive from an economic point of view, while the remaining processes of internal investment had been perversely influenced toward speculative ventures in non-productive wealth.

Additional Impact of Growing Needs

The system's inability to fulfill the requirements of economic development became more pronounced with the changing nature and the increasing number of new needs and aspirations of the people. Total requirements grew rapidly with the increment of the population, at the same time that needs multiplied as a consequence of greater contact established over the years with societies enjoying much wider and diversified patterns of consumption.

This demonstration effect was not confined to the consumption of goods and services. New ideas were brought in after World War I emphasizing that crisis and stagnation could be avoided and that higher standards of living were not the exclusive privilege of certain countries or certain classes. Contact with these ideas enhanced the dissatisfaction with the performance of the economy and contributed to the emergence of widespread social ferments throughout Central America. They erupted occasionally in popular uprisings, as in El Salvador in 1932, and in strong strike movements, as in Costa Rica in 1934.

There followed a period of government by new strong men in Nicaragua, Honduras, El Salvador and Guatemala which was to last generally until 1944-48. During that period, roughly corresponding to that of the long crisis, they were able to maintain a certain measure of public order by forcefully containing the upheavals that threatened to upset the traditional organizations of government, economy, and social classes. Things evolved differently in Costa Rica, where, because of the long-standing tradition of social equality and the existing relative dispersion of economic power, the consequences of the crisis did not lead to the supression of the effective functioning of the institutions of political democracy. However, it is interesting to note that it was precisely in this country that the first measures for a fundamental alteration of the traditional economic and social system were taken in the early 1940's, comprising the broad field of labor legislation, social security, higher education, and the beginnings of an agrarian reform.

Recent Variations Around a Stagnant Pattern

The evolution of the Central American export economy during the postwar period confirms the proposition that the first stage of economic development came to an end in these countries in the early 1930's. Because of the slow increase in the volume of exports, the increment of total production in the region barely covered population growth during most of the period of high export prices (1947-54). As noted in the previous chapter, the rate of growth slowed down after 1955, when export prices fell and unemployment and idle capacity increased. The policies followed to cope with this crisis were reasonably successful in maintaining both external equilibrium and internal price stability. But they could not achieve sustained economic development, even at the rather low rates experienced in the early 1950's.

Although they could not quite escape the effects of the crisis, investment in manufacturing and industrial output grew at fairly rapid rates during this decade, always exceeding the average rates for the economy as a whole.[13] However, this sector was not capable of absorbing the natural growth of urban population. In addition to the factors mentioned earlier, the continuing inability to generate a vigorous process of industrialization in Central America must be attributed to the decisive limitations rooted into the small extent of five weakened and fragmented national markets. By contrast, the larger Latin American countries, with bigger markets, found themselves in a better position to promote industrial development and import substitution as they emerged out of the depression of 1930's.

Some gains were recorded in the agricultural sector for the domestic market; they were mostly in new products, furnishing raw materials for the canning and processed food industries. But the production of the main staples (corn, rice and beans), representing the larger portion of domestic agriculture, remained untouched and continued to grow at a very slow pace. Moreover, the inroads of cotton into subsistence agriculture worsened the already precarious equilibrium of the food and export sectors in the countries that became substantial producers of this fiber, notably, Nicaragua and El Salvador.

For these reasons, the postwar years must be considered as a period of variations around a basically stagnant pattern. Low export prices and business crises recurred, whereas the positive changes were neither big, nor deep, enough to reestablish the functioning of the agricultural export economy as a permanent nucleus of growth.

Footnotes to Chapter 6

1. For an analysis of long-term trends in the world coffee market, see Di Fulvio, op. cit., pp. 112-113, 513 and 520-26; also FAO, La Economia Mundial del Café, Serie sobre productos No. 33 (Rome, 1961), pp. 25-27, 30-32, 36-39 and 55. The data on trends in the banana market are taken from: J. Wolf, "Evolución y Estructura del Mercado Bananero Mundial," Boletín Mensual de Economía y Estadística Agrícola, Vol. VIII, No. 2 (Rome, FAO, February 1959), pp. 7-8.

2. United Nations, "The International Banana Market - Its Evolution and Prospects," Economic Bulletin for Latin America, op. cit., pp. 17-26.

3. For an account of the present number and diversity of such restrictions, see United Nations, Economic Commission for Latin America, América Latina y la Conferencia de las Naciones Unidas sobre Comercio y Desarrollo (Santiago, Chile, 1964), pp. 87-115.

4. L. Baranyai and J. C. Mills, Convenios de Estabilización de las Materias Primas (Mexico City: CEMLA, 1962), p. 148.

5. Ibid., pp. 145-158.

6. Di Fulvio, op. cit., p. 112, and FAO, La Economía Mundial del Café, op. cit., p. 61.

7. J. Wolf, op. cit., p. 7.

8. According to the official statistics published in the Foreign Trade Yearbooks of the respective countries.

9. See International Bank for Reconstruction and Development and International Development Association, The Commodity Problem, Report No. EC-129, Staff Study of the Economic Department (Washington, D. C., May 1964), Annex 1, p. 3.

10. Rodrigo Facio, La Moneda y la Banca Central en Costa Rica (Mexico City: Fondo de Cultura Económica, 1947), pp. 161-215; Soley Güell, op. cit., Vol. I, pp. 282-283, Vol. II, pp. 52, 110, 135-145, 278-284. Solórzano Fernández, op. cit., pp. 329-340; Young, op. cit., pp. 121-130, and Banco Central de Nicaragua, Primer Informe Anual, 1961 (Managua), pp. 4-5.

11. See Henry Wallich and John H. Adler, Proyecciones Económicas de las Finanzas Públicas: Un Estudio Experimental en El Salvador, Fondo de Cultura Económica (Mexico City, 1949), pp. 217-237.

12. Felix Choussy, Actual Panorama Económico Agrícola de El Salvador (Ministry of Agriculture, San Salvador, 1952), p. 6.

13. United Nations, Economic Commission for Latin America, Los Problemas de la Política Industrial Centroamericana, (E/CN.12/CCE/311), (Mexico City, 1964), pp. 5-6.

PART II

SEARCH FOR A NEW PATTERN OF GROWTH

CHAPTER **7** THE CASE FOR
ECONOMIC INTEGRATION
IN CENTRAL AMERICA

From Past to Present History

To examine the initial experiences gained in Central America's
economic integration,to analyze the problems arising from the
operations of the common market,and to try to anticipate the future
course of the region's actions toward economic union are the main
purposes of this part of the study. In so doing, a different analytical
approach will have to be used. Whereas the first part has dealt with
the larger processes leading to the organization of an economic system
and, in broad outline, with the latter's quantitative characteristics and
evolution as an ongoing concern, the following chapters will be
centered mainly on actions needed to construct a new pattern of growth
and on the more detailed and specific questions, largely of a qualitative nature, that emerge in this context. This will be an attempt to
gain insight into the future transformation of an economy and not an
evaluation of the performance of an already established system.

Up to this point, the present study has referred to a time span of
one century, while the Central American experience in economic
integration so far covers only little more than a decade. Problems and
perspectives, therefore, will of necessity be different. It is relatively
easy to engage with detachment in an interpretation of the first stage
of these countries' economic development, since this is largely a matter
of past history. It is difficult to do the same with respect to the living
questions of the present; for it implies taking a position on the relative
significance of these questions and on alternative measures to be
adopted in the future.

Allowing for the changes that have taken place in the intervening decades, this part of the study is thus more akin to one that might have been written a century ago, when the Central American countries were also in need of a new pattern of growth. However, its substantive relationship with the first part of this study will be noted. For the behavior of societies, economic or otherwise, is always strongly rooted in their history and, if continued progress is to be achieved, the future can ignore the past only at its own peril.

The Need for Economic Reconstruction

The reconstruction of the national economies, in accordance with a new pattern of growth, arose in the postwar period as a paramount need in Central America. The first stage of growth had allowed for appreciable improvements in the levels of living of the population and contributed to the development of valuable human and natural resources. It had also enabled the various countries to establish links with the modern world of culture and economy and to define their identity among contemporary nations with a certain measure of success.

But, having exhausted the main possibilities of export agriculture, it has become necessary to reorganize the productive apparatus and to expand it along the lines of a parallel restructuring of products and factors markets. This would make it possible for the countries of the region to consolidate the gains already achieved, to propagate the process of growth to their backward areas, to overcome the structural imbalances of their economies, and to provide a new thrust for continued progress in the future.

It is not easy to conceive such a task in all its complexities. Historically, there are not many cases in which a community has fully grasped the nature and significance of a problem of this kind, and the few instances that are known seem to have occurred in the face of a fundamental and immediate external threat to their survival. Usually, the total reorganization of an economy has been achieved in a less spectacular fashion, through partial changes that eventually give new dimensions to the productive system. This was the way in which multinational co-operation was originally envisaged by the Latin American governments[1] and, to this day, gradual change has characterized the Central American economic integration efforts.

Partly for this reason, as well as others to be mentioned presently, this study does not aim to examine the theoretical arguments that may justify regional integration as an essential condition for the reconstruction of the Central American economies. Its point of departure is the fact that there is a process of economic integration already under way among the five countries. Whether or not they would be wise to follow alternative courses of action is regarded here as an academic question, although the author is not unaware that analyses of a purely economic nature have failed thus far to prove conclusively the general case for economic integration.[2] However, one cannot avoid the issue of whether there are firm grounds justifying the case for economic integration in Central America and a judgement, however tentative, must be established as to the ways in which it can contribute to the solution of the basic problems that confront the individual countries in the second half of the twentieth century.

The Historical Basis of Economic Integration

The issue begins to be joined by inquiring whether, and in what ways, the ideal of Central American union can serve as the historical element on which to ground a multinational scheme of economic integration. It is true that searching doubts were raised throughout the nineteenth century as to the viability of these countries as politically independent states, and that at various times some of their more eminent citizens considered, and even explored, the possibilities of annexation to a larger power.[3] Experience with the relatively successful assertion of their sovereignty and the subsequent development of their economic systems helped to dispel such doubts. At the same time an awareness of the need to re-establish the Central American union survived the disintegration of the federal republic and has been shared by the five countries up to the present time. This awareness and several facts, mainly of a political nature, have led their governments into repeated efforts toward the reconstruction of regional unity.

There have been four major instances: The so-called "República Mayor" between 1896 and 1898; the Washington Treaties of 1910; the Federal Republic of Central America in 1921, and the Organization of Central American States (ODECA) established in 1951.[4] Some of those efforts were prompted, among other things, by the need to protect the countries from foreign domination. This was the case of the "Republica Mayor," growing out of concern caused by the prospect of a British invasion in Nicaragua; it was also the case of the Central American

Court of Justice, adopted as a mechanism to settle disputes among member countries, without having to submit to the intervention of foreign powers. Others developed as efforts to eliminate internal political strife, such as the Washington Treaty of Peace and Friendship, and all of them arose as so many expressions of the ideal of Central American union.[5]

The failure of the first three attempts and ODECA's limited performance to date do not detract in any way from the merits and breadth of vision of those who organized them and who gave their energies to make them a success. They saw that union was a key factor to secure the sovereignty of their countries and that only by joining efforts could they hope to build a respected place in the concert of nations. Nevertheless, these failures hold important lessons. They show that the distance is long between the formulation of an objective and its realization, that ideals of this kind provide no more than a very broad orientation, and that action programs have to be developed with direct reference to the materials available in the situation as it exists.

Most of the efforts were made long before the end of the first stage of Central American development, when the traditional export economy still provided the basis for a fairly satisfactory process of growth. In this respect, therefore, the existing economic situation was over-whelmingly oriented toward the outside, and was not conducive to a different, multinational pattern. There was also a substantial lack of knowledge about how to put the ideal to work; how to proceed in the task of reaching stated purposes. Even a cursory review of the treaties reveals that their objectives were so broad as to give little guidance to implementation; that as regards their execution, they included no more than simple lists of things to be done, failing in nearly all cases to provide ways and means to accomplish and secure them. There was the added fact that the efforts occasionally comprised only three of the five countries, as was true in 1896 and in 1921. And even these partial attempts were brought quickly to an end as a result of sudden changes of government in the participating countries.

However, not everything was lost in the process. For it is on the basis of this stubborn persistence, and in the face of recurrent foreign trade crises, that the ideal of Central American union has acquired a new and more relevant meaning in the economic sphere.

An increasing awareness of the breakdown of multilateralism in the world economy and of the chronic crises in the markets for agricultural exports has naturally led to an examination of the possibilities of growth within the national markets, and later within the larger regional market. The efforts exerted in other parts of the world to cope with the imbalances originating from the emergence of a few superpowers, through regional groupings such as the European Economic Community, provided an example to be followed in certain respects. Moreover, the creation of these economic power blocks and the tendency of larger industrialized countries to grow inward has dampened whatever impetus there might have been for the Central American countries to continue to view their economic fate in terms of an exclusively national connection with the centers of income and wealth.

Similar and closely related considerations of an internal nature have served to buttress the case for Central American economic integration. In addition to the vivid experience of a long period of instability, the awareness that economic growth can be wilfully achieved and that its promotion constitutes a public responsibility has provided the starting point in this endeavor.

Initially, this found expression in the substantial policy and institutional developments of the postwar period that were mentioned in the previous chapter (establishment of central banks and development corporations, social legislation, tariff policy, etc.), as well as in the relatively large public works programs and private business investments that have been carried out with a view to realizing the potentialities of the internal economies. The very success of these initial business ventures spurred the search for additional markets within the region and gave rise to the negotiation of a series of bilateral trade agreements among the five countries in the early 1950's. Moreover, the experience of some of the larger Latin American countries had shown to the Central Americans that industrial development was feasible if it could count on adequate domestic markets. As a result of these experiences and changing outlooks, it was not difficult to visualize the way in which the ideal of Central American union might be put to work in the economic field, so as to enhance the national development efforts through intraregional trade and specialization of productive activity.

Thus, a wider horizon of opportunities emerged gradually, within a new psychological and ideological environment which, without entailing major discontinuities with the historical background, has begun to reorient the economic development of the countries of the region. Functionally, such an environment performs the same role as that which, in its time, gave rise to the agricultural export economy. But it is aimed now to the development of an urban, industrialized society, rather than of a rural, raw material producing economy. Taking the long view, it is interesting to note how the same kind of factors that led to an economic organization along national lines in the nineteenth century should have operated in the opposite direction one hundred years later, toward the creation of a productive system of regional scope.

The preceding considerations lead to the conclusion that historical factors are favorable to the economic union of the Central American countries. To put it the other way around, the changes that have taken place during the past three decades, particularly as regards Central America's economic relations with the outside world, tend to give greater sway to the historical ties among the five countries, so as to strengthen their economic integration. This is not to say that politically divisive forces cannot arise in the future, that may slow down or even destroy the integration effort. What can be said with some degree of confidence, however, is that the Central American economic union has greater chances of succeeding than one composed of a more hetero-geneous group of countries with weaker historical relationships; for example, an economic association of any one or several of the Central American countries with neighboring nations, such as Colombia, Mexico, or Venezuela.

Economic Integration and the Problems of Central American Development

The other side of the issue under scrutiny calls for an appraisal of the relationship between economic integration and the main economic problems facing the five countries, as well as of the extent to which such an approach can contribute to their solution. In this case, the actual experiences of the past decade are too scant to provide conclusive evidence. Nevertheless, there are some grounds upon which it is possible to anticipate, prima facie, a hopeful answer.

On the basis of the analyses developed in Part I of this study, the terms of the problems faced by the Central American countries at the present time may be reduced to two basic questions: (a) the need to restructure the traditional links of these countries with the international economy and (b) the need to effect the internal adjustments that are required for this and other purposes, including those related with the

existing structural disequilibria and those that will be called for in
connection with the fulfillment of new economic opportunities. These
two basic questions involve, among others, the well known problems
of investment, diversification of production and resource development,
on the one hand, and the strengthening of internal demand and more
effective access to the external markets for new and traditional exports,
on the other.

Theoretically, the relationship between economic integration and
the possible solution of these problems has been formulated in terms of
the way in which such a process contributes to overcoming the limitations arising out of the small size of the national markets and enables
the participating countries to reap the greater benefits of external
economies and economies of scale.[6] The question, therefore, is
whether the Central American countries fit this general case.

Considered individually, their territorial dimensions (ranging
between 8,000 and 40,000 square miles), the size of their populations
(between 1.5 and 4.5 million people) and the magnitude of their total
purchasing power (from 500 millions to little over 1 billion dollars
yearly), all lead to an obviously positive answer to the query. Moreover, this seems to be confirmed by the available judgement, based on
the experience of industrialized countries. According to such judgment,
the achievement of significant economies of scale--in a broad sense
--requires a minimum national market of between 10 to 15 million
people.[7]

Specific studies and experiences in Central America have resulted
in more precise information to the same effect. Thus, it has been shown
that the consolidated regional market would make it possible to enlarge
the size of existing plants, to specialize product mixes and to modernize
equipment so as to obtain substantial gains in efficiency and competitive conditions in several manufacturing activities already established.[8]
Moreover, the initial experiences of the common market have proved in
actual practice the possibility of launching new industries--such as
fertilizers, insecticides, caustic soda, tires--as well as service facilities and light engineering plants, that could not have been established
as self-sustained operations within the narrow economic and geographic
boundaries of any of the five countries.

In agriculture the situation is not as well known as in manufacturing,
partly because it has received less attention in the integration program.
Several studies have pointed out that a multinational economic unit

could lead to important gains in efficiency through specialization tied more closely to the ecological characteristics of the region as a whole. This would require a readjustment of the existing man-land ratios, the consolidation of the present fragmented markets and the pooling of the available technical and financial resources in a truly joint effort of regional scope.[9] Thus far, intraregional trade has made it possible to maintain a reasonable degree of self-sufficiency in food staples under conditions of low or moderate rates of growth. The expanded market has also spurred the production of vegetable oils, and plans are under way for attaining self-sufficiency in milk products by 1970. The modernization of domestic agriculture, however, is still in its initial stage, and substantial gains in the productivity of this sector will have to be achieved, in order to sustain rapid industrial development and the urbanization of the economy.

This, of course, will also depend on the speed and efficiency with which the required infrastructural facilities can be constructed. Here again, studies have shown that a multinational approach to the development of electric power would give rise to significant economies of scale in both hydro and thermal generation. This entails the construction of an interconnected system of plants of a size that could not be justified for a long time to come on the basis of the national markets taken in isolation. The same is true of the possible development for multipurpose use of certain international rivers and high potential watersheds.[10]

Similar conditions may characterize the situation in the transportation sector. Here the increasing volume of intraregional trade and the lengthening of transportation leads will soon warrant the increased utilization of heavier vehicles, equipment and cheaper fuels, so as to take advantage of the opportunities offered by the larger and rapidly growing common market.

Finally, preliminary feasibility projects have shown that the construction of a telecommunications network, with a view to serving the national and regional needs and to functioning as a link between the southern and northern countries of the hemisphere, could greatly increase the efficiency of this service and reduce its cost to consumers.[11] Thus it is fair to anticipate that, in Central America, economic integration would tend to effect a significant improvement in the general cost conditions of the economy as a whole.

Broader Economic Implications of
a Regional Approach

If further probing and additional experience were to confirm the
above-mentioned possibilities, their implications would be important
for the main supply and demand problems facing the five countries at
this stage of their economic history. Thus, regional integration could
substantially strengthen internal demand not only by widening, but also
by deepening the extent of the market. This would be effected in terms
of its sheer impact upon internal economic activity, through import
substitution and inducements to other productive opportunities in
general, and of the real possibility of freeing thereby the agricultural
and construction industries from the limitations of balance of payments
bottlenecks. In addition, internal demand could also be strengthened,
if the political advantages of a multinational over a purely national
approach were utilized to promote the generalization and improvement
of existing schemes of social insurance, labor legislations,and the
development of other aspects of an incomes policy based upon suitable
minimum wage, tax, price,and land reform programs.

Given the relatively small size of the common market, Central
America will continue to rely heavily on commodity exports as a basis
for sustained growth. Hence, internal changes will have to be accompanied by vigorous joint efforts to redefine the region's commercial policy
vis-à-vis third countries, so as to make possible the expansion and
diversification of exports. Economic integration cannot do this job by
itself. But it can help Central America to conduct its external
economic affairs more effectively by lowering general cost levels and
improving its competitive position, by enhancing through joint efforts the
capabilities for physical and economic performances, and by
strengthening its bargaining position in the international context.

Obviously, these developments would bear a direct relationship
with other aspects of the region's patterns of economy. The emergence
of different types of stimuli for investment in new productive lines
entails a qualitative change in the perspectives of entrepreneurs,
investors,and governments. Conditions might then be propitious for
lessening the preponderance of traditional activities, as well as
overcoming other obstacles to change that are implicit in the functioning
of the economic systems taken in isolation.

Thus, the process of diversification of productive activity would
contribute to the provision of remunerative employment to a labor force

that for more than three decades has not found adequate opportunities. It would also propagate economic growth to those areas of the economy which were bypassed in the developmental impulse of the nineteenth century.

A simple comparison with the hypothesis of an alternative, purely national effort to accomplish identical objectives leads to the conclusion that, in addition to its being viable and efficient, economic integration may well constitute a necessary condition to solve the basic economic problems faced by the five countries. For, in general, a system that is geared to a particular pattern of economy is not likely to function effectively in accordance with a different, larger, and more complex pattern of economy. To this extent, economic integration would provide an opportunity for the Central Americans to flex their muscles, so to speak, and to develop the capabilities required to strengthen their position in the world economy.

If this is true, economic integration is not simply one of several equally relevant possibilities. It represents rather a course of action that excludes other alternatives, such as the isolated action of individual countries. In its initial stages it is not, to be sure, a substitute but a supplement to what already exists. This is amply demonstrated by the fact that traditional exports and total imports from outside the area have been growing rapidly in recent years, along with similar rises in intraregional trade.

But as time elapses, economic integration may turn out to be not simply the addition of new economic elements side by side with the traditional sectors, but rather the source of a far reaching process of total adjustment. In this sense, economic integration involves changes in the form taken by national action and in the strategy for attacking the problem of economic development, with a peculiarly different sequence of operations and priorities, that begin by establishing the legal and institutional framework for the new multinational unit, and then proceed along a parallel path of import substitution and reorganization and expansion of the relationships with the rest of the world.

Although it may be necessary, economic integration is not, however, a sufficient condition for the solution of Central America's basic economic problems. It is hoped that the previous analyses have been clear in showing that economic integration is but a form of structuring an effort that facilitates the introduction of change in the existing systems. As such, it conditions internal organizational reforms as well as investment and productive processes, by enhancing the opportunities for growth. In this sense, economic integration is intermediate and instrumental, not final and conclusive.

If the required changes and reforms are not effected, no common market will in and of itself make for a new stage of growth; and the Central American countries would have succeeded only in joining hands for continued stagnation and insufficiencies. But if they are effected, the Central Americans could look forward to a process of vigorous growth that would enable them to discharge their responsibilities in a world which is beginning to grow aware of the burden of too many small countries of dubious viability.

Footnotes to Chapter 7

1. United Nations, Economic Commission for Latin America, Informe sobre el Tercer Período de Sesiones (E/1717) (New York, 1949), pp. 13 and 18.

2. E. A. Robinson (ed.), Economic Consequences of the Size of Nations, Proceedings of Conference held by the International Economic Association (London: MacMillan & Co., Ltd., 1960).

3. Karnes, op. cit., pp. 20-8; Carr, op. cit., p. 50.

4. For a documentary account of these and other attempts, see Alberto Herrarte, Documentos de la Unión Centroamericana (Guatemala: Editorial del Ministerio de Educación Pública, 1957).

5. Torres, op. cit., pp. 114-33.

6. See, for example, Bela Balassa, The Theory of Economic Integration (London: George Allen & Unwin Ltd., 1961) and Sidney Dell, Trade Blocks and Common Markets (London: Constable, 1963).

7. Robinson, op. cit., pp. xvii-xviii.

8. See, for example, United Nations, Economic Commission for Latin America, Programa de desarrollo de la industria de hilados y tejidos de algodón en Centroamérica (E/CN.12/CCE/356; TAO/LAT/57) (Mexico City, 1966, /mimeographed/.

9. United Nations, Economic Commission for Latin America, "Evaluación y perspectivas del Programa de Integración Económica de Centroamérica," Boletín Económico de América Latina, Vol. IV, No.2 (Santiago, Chile, October, 1959), pp. 42-4 and Evaluación de la Integración Económica en Centroamérica (E/CN.12/CCE/327/Rev. 1) (Mexico City, 1966), pp. 79-95, /mimeographed/.

10. United Nations, Economic Commission for Latin America, La política regional de energía en Centroamérica (E/CN.12/CCE/SC.5/41; TAO/LAT/63) (Mexico City, 1966), /mimeographed/.

11. United Nations Special Fund, Estudio sobre la Red Regional de Telecomunicaciones entre las Repúblicas del Istmo Centroamericano (2 vols. and appendices, New York, 1964).

8 THE PROGRAM
FOR ECONOMIC
INTEGRATION

Origin and Evolution of the Program

The first successful experiences in the reconstruction of Central
American unity were not achieved until the early 1950's, when the
program for economic integration was launched. A different approach
was used this time. Instead of superimposing the ultimate objectives of
political federation upon several centrifugal systems, the attempt now
was to add to them a real dimension of regional scope in the form of
a series of common, newly created economic interests. Instead of
a total movement toward immediate union, the sights were set upon
a more limited, less inclusive target. The chances for union in the
future were thus grounded on the consolidation of national markets and
their gradual transformation and growth as a single economic unit.

An important circumstance existed in 1950, in addition to those
mentioned in the previous chapter, that was favorable to the integration movement: A new generation, more concerned with the
realities of economic growth than with the niceties of diplomacy or the
rhetorics of political union, had reached positions of power in the
governments of the five countries. It was the vision of these men that
enabled them to see far ahead and to conceive the economic integration
program, in spite of the complacent mood encouraged by the high
export prices prevailing at the time.

Supported by the traditional ideal of Central American union and
by the combination of all of these circumstances, the five governments
agreed in 1951 to engage in a program to promote the "gradual and
progressive" integration of their countries' national economies. During
the Fourth Session of the United Nations Economic Commission for

Latin America, held in Mexico City, the Central American Economic Co-operation Committee (CCE) was established to take charge of the program, and the United Nations was called upon to provide it with advisory services. The ministers of Economy were designated ex-officio members of the CCE. The Committee was set up as a body of the Economic Commission for Latin America (ECLA). Advisory and secretariat services were provided by the ECLA Secretariat and technical assistance rendered by the United Nations and its specialized agencies, such as FAO and ILO.[1]

It is to be noted that the integration program was launched by means of a simple resolution, without fanfare and without the signature of any formal treaty. Yet it was to be the most successful joint effort in the region since independence. By 1966, the five countries could point to solid achievements: A free trade area, which has been in operation for five years; a common external tariff on nearly all import items; and three Central American institutions for the administration of the common market and the orientation of the integration program, the Economic Council, the Executive Council and the Permanent Secretariat.

The five governments have established also the Central American Economic Integration Bank (BCIE), operating since 1961, whose credit resources amount now to nearly 100 million dollars; an institute for technological and industrial research (ICAITI), which has worked with the private sector and the national development institutions for ten years; and a school of public administration (ESAPAC), which for more than one decade has carried the task of upgrading the governments' administrative ranks, especially in fields related to the integration program, including customs administration, administration of fiscal incentives and, more recently, administration of development programs.

There are three basic legal instruments in the common market: The General Treaty on Central American Economic Integration (1960), the Multilateral Treaty on Central American Free Trade and Economic Integration (1958) and the Central American Agreement on Tariff Equalization (1959) and its protocols (1959, 1960, 1962, 1964, 1965). In addition, there are two instruments on customs legislation and administration: The Central American Uniform Customs Code (1963) and the Central American Uniform Tariff Nomenclature (1953). Two other treaties--the Agreement on the Regime of Central American Integration Industries (1958) and its protocols (1963, 1965) and the Agreement on Fiscal Incentives for Industrial Development (1962)--cover specific aspects of regional industrial policy. In the area of transportation, three Central American laws regulate highway traffic (1958), road signs and signals,and temporary imports of motor vehicles (1956).[2]

The program has also developed in other directions. The central banks have successfully set up a clearing house to settle payments for intraregional trade[3] and have agreed to move toward the gradual establishment of a Central American monetary union. Several regional investment programs are under way at different stages of implementation, mainly in the fields of road construction, telecommunications, interconnection of electric power systems and building of storage facilities for agricultural products.[4] The five national universities are tackling the problems of higher education and scientific research with a regional approach, in an attempt to strengthen their action through joint operations and specialization. The task of reconstruction of external trade policy, now as a regional enterprise, is already in the preparatory stage. At the same time, an increasing number of government departments and agencies are beginning to participate in the affairs of economic integration--Ministries of Finance, Agriculture, Education, Public Health and Labor; Social Security, Development, Housing, Tourism and Electrification institutes--, while the private sectors are organizing themselves at the regional level in order to further their growing commercial and industrial interests within the common market.

The Common Market: Basic Issues

Two distinct phases may be differentiated in the early stages of the program for economic integration. The first, between 1952 and 1957,was one of incubation, examination and confrontation of possibilities, assessment of possible consequences,and accumulation of limited experiences. The second phase, 1958 through 1962, was one of rapid progress and of far reaching achievements.

From the standpoint of economic planning and more generally of the tasks that economists are called upon to perform as advisers in questions of public policy, it is of more than passing importance to note that during these ten years the main concern was not the definition of basic objectives. The task was rather one of clarifying questions of implementation, of how to go about accomplishing the already stated objective of a common market, in terms which were at once economically meaningful and politically viable. No attempt was made to define objectives in terms of what to produce, how much and under what technical relationships; the purpose was at all times to discover the legal framework to be established, within which accommodation and expansion of economic activity could proceed at a reasonably fast pace and with as few major disturbances as possible.

The first phase fulfilled two purposes: (a) to establish the program as an ongoing endeavor, and (b) to gain knowledge and sharpen the issues concerning the common market. The first purpose required the development of an effective mechanism, including a close-knit group of government officials who could provide for continuity of effort and help create a regional point of view for approaching the problems involved. The Committee on Economic Co-operation (CCE) grew up to be that kind of a mechanism, and its Trade Subcommittee just that kind of a group. Stable in its composition over a period of years, the latter group contributed in no small way to the development of a regional point of view. At the same time, adequate relationships were established between the governments at various levels and the United Nations agencies; it was then possible to utilize external co-operation for the study of economic integration problems with a reasonable degree of efficiency.

A capacity to produce concrete achievements at an early date helped secure the program as an ongoing concern. It was during this period that the Central American School of Public Administration (ESAPAC) and the Central American Technological and Industrial Research Institute (ICAITI) were established (1954-55). To be sure, these institutions were not geared at the time to any specific process of economic integration; rather they were the upshot of a pragmatic approach wherein the first available opportunities for joint action were grasped and carried out. The continuity of the program was thus helped by the psychological lift they created, as well as by their intrinsic meaning as first multinational commitments. The regional status given to these institutions prevented their proliferation at the national level. This enhanced the possibilities for the member countries to improve their administrative personnel and to absorb technological knowledge more effectively. Later on, as the program unfolded, they could be linked more closely to the specific needs of economic integration.

Getting to know the issues involved in the creation of the common market required a substantial amount of research on the problems and characteristics of the five national economies, and on the scope and nature of the measures that might be taken for that purpose. This research work resulted in a series of major studies--the first ever to be attempted in these countries on a systematic basis--on general development, transportation, agriculture, electric power, taxation, commercial policy and industrial possibilities.[5] They ranged from country development studies, to sectoral research, resource surveys and, in some cases, the formulation of specific investment projects. They provided information for policy decisions and clarified some of the issues involved.

At the same time, practical experience was being obtained through a system of bilateral trade treaties. El Salvador had taken the initiative in this field around 1950, and within a decade a complete network was established tying all five countries. In addition, the adoption of a common tariff nomenclature[6] greatly facilitated the subsequent task of negotiating the free trade and tariff equalization agreements.

A cohesive group of government officials, a continuous flow of external technical assistance, a series of systematic studies, and an increasing experience with the problems of free trade: These were the main elements in the search for a solution to the common market question.

Free Trade under the Multilateral Treaty of 1958

Two intimately related issues defined the basic terms of the question: (a) what mechanisms and procedures could perform more efficiently in freeing trade within the region as much and as rapidly as possible, and (b) how could such mechanisms and procedures be fitted into the national systems so as to minimize or to correct the disturbances that were likely to occur as a result of free trade and tariff equalization. In evaluating alternative formulas, as much or more time was devoted to the question of their repercussions on the established national economies as was devoted to consideration of their efficiency in creating a common market.

Concern about the disturbances centered around three possible effects of free trade: (a) losses of government revenues, as goods would enter each country from the other duty free; (b) unfavorable impact upon existing productive activities in some countries, as they began to face stiffer competition from the same industries in other member countries, and (c) concentration of new industries in one or two countries, as a result simply of their being already farther ahead than the rest in their relative degree of development, or of "artificial" differences in national policy instruments, such as the external tariffs

and the tax incentive laws for industrial development. It can easily be
seen that, other things being equal, there was a direct relationship
between the legal and institutional scope of the common market and
these sources of concern. Hence the more sweeping the free trade
proposals, the larger did their national repercussions loom in the minds
of decision makers.

This explains why the Treaty on Multilateral Free Trade (1958),
though broad in its final objectives, was cautious as to the means of
attaining them. Under this Treaty the five countries agreed to establish
a free trade zone in their territories over a maximum period of ten
years, and granted immediate free trade or preferential treatment to the
Central American products included in a small attached list. The free
trade zone was to be perfected--in the GATT sense of according
national treatment to a substantial fraction of their reciprocal trade
--by means of periodic multilateral negotiations designed to incorpo-
rate additional products in the original list.[7]

In addition, the Multilateral Treaty included provisions on subsidies to intraregional exports, trade discrimination, transit of goods
among countries, transport and communications,and national treatment
to investments originating in the member countries. Certain clauses
made it possible to compensate for the possible loss of revenue from
import duties by permitting the establishment of nondiscriminatory
internal consumption taxes. A Central American Trade Commission,
made up of representatives from the five governments, was created for
the purpose of administering and perfecting the free trade zone,
together with various related matters having to do with the expansion of
the economic integration movement. This Commission was superseded
later, in the General Treaty, by the Economic and Executive Councils
and by the Permanent Secretariat.

The Multilateral Trade Treaty is very similar to the Montevideo
Treaty signed in 1960, which created the Latin American Free Trade
Association (LAFTA) comprising, originally, Argentina, Brazil, Chile,
Mexico, Paraguay, Peru and Uruguay. The similarity refers especially
to the way in which the free trade zone was defined in concrete terms
and to the basic procedures which were adopted for its achievement.
Thus, the GATT concept of a trade-freeing process covering a substantial fraction of reciprocal trade was defined as the objective of the
Montevideo Treaty, and a twelve year period was agreed upon to
perfect this process, by means of periodic, product-by-product
negotiations.[8]

However, there are several differences between the two instruments. In addition to its somewhat shorter transition period, the Multilateral Treaty went directly into a system of permanent free trade, as
agreed in the product lists, instead of the two-step procedure of
national (provisional) and common (permanent) lists envisaged in
Montevideo.[9]

There are differences also in the approach taken to the problem of
balanced development among countries. Thus, the LAFTA Treaty
permits the less developed countries to proceed according to a slower
schedule of trade liberalization, to enjoy exceptions to the
most-favored-nation clause and to protect national production under
certain conditions.[10] The Central Americans, on the other hand,
attempted to provide for equitable distribution of benefits among
countries by agreeing in the treaty on integration industries, that
manufacturing activities requiring access to the regional market for
their establishment would be located by intergovernmental decision,
and free trade and other privileges would be granted to these industries
under specifically stipulated conditions.[11]

It is apparent from what has been said that in the Multilateral
Treaty the objective of rapid liberalization of trade gave way to the
need to minimize disturbances. Each member country could safeguard
her interests as she saw fit simply by avoiding, in the process of
negotiations, the inclusion of any item in the free trade list. Moreover,
by spreading the negotiations over a ten year period, without a stipulated rate of progress, ample opportunity was given to acquire experience with the new device of multilateral free trade.

Tariff Equalization

One reason why it was not possible in 1958 to agree on a more
rapid system of freeing intraregional trade was the lack of a parallel
commitment as regards tariff equalization. Experience shows that the
broader the scope of trade liberalization, the more important it becomes
for the participating countries to have uniform duties on imports from the
outside world. It is obvious that in a free trade area built upon
diverging national tariffs, free trade tends to benefit more the countries
with the lower duties, while those with the higher rates may be
confronted with difficulties arising from illegal transfer of goods
originating outside the area.

Although at the time the import tariffs of the Central American countries still followed the traditional orientation of revenue-producing rates fixed at relatively low levels, the situation prevailing in 1958 was mixed enough already as to warrant a concern for tariff equalization as a condition for rapid progress in freeing intraregional trade. Moreover, most of the countries were aware of the need to restructure their tariffs and to adjust them to the requirements of balance of payments policy and industrial development. Finally, the absence of monetary and foreign exchange controls, of the type prevalent in many LAFTA countries, facilitated the negotiations leading to a single import tariff for Central America.

Thus, in 1959, the five governments were able to sign the Central American Agreement on Tariff Equalization, calling for the establishment of a common tariff on imports from outside the region within a maximum period of five years. This was to be done through periodic, item-by-item negotiations, whose results would be formalized in additional protocols to the basic Agreement. [12]

For this purpose quantitative guidelines were adopted, so as to fix the total incidence of the specific and advalorem components of the various duties within given ranges specifying minimum and maximum levels for different categories of goods. These were low or negligible for capital goods, raw materials, and other production goods not produced in the region; moderate for products, mainly consumer goods, not susceptible of production in the area; and relatively high for goods produced in Central America or which could be easily developed in the short run. Fiscal and balance of payments considerations were also utilized in certain cases.

The pertinent guidelines were then applied to each of thirty-two commodity groups in which the tariff nomenclature was arranged, following economic criteria. This made it possible to bring together within the same group or industry larger numbers of products related among themselves as raw materials, intermediate, final or substitute goods, thus introducing a more rational structure into the tariff instrument. On this basis, duties were finally fixed through multilateral negotiations and with the aid of statistical information on internal production, imports, prices, the height of the corresponding national tariffs and the like.

In general the common duties went into effect upon ratification of the corresponding protocols. However, in cases that involved substantial

changes from the pre-existing national tariffs, the uniform duty could
be reached gradually, over a maximum period of five years, in
accordance with predetermined conditions as to the length of the
transition period, rates of change,and points of departure for the
equalization process.[13]

All of this was required in order to remove uncertainties as to the
way in which uniform rates were to be reached. Moreover, it was
necessary to arrive at a common tariff structure that would not require
fundamental revisions in the short run. For such revisions entail new
multilateral negotiations and ratification by the legislatures of the
member countries. This procedure differs from the one adopted in the
East African Common Market where, in the absence of a legally
binding multilateral commitment, import duties can be altered unilaterally, subject only to an intergovernmental de facto consultation of an
informal nature.[14]

Simpler methods could have been used in arriving at a common
import tariff. In the European Economic Community (EEC), for example,
the arithmetic average of the pre-existing national duties has been
widely used to fix the level of uniform rates.[15] The procedures and
criteria used in Central America responded to the need of devising
a new tariff instrument which, in addition to its traditional revenue-
producing and balance-of-payments functions, could serve mainly as
a stimulus to industrial development.

By 1965, uniform import duties had been established on practically
all (98 per cent) of the items in the common tariff nomenclature. It is
interesting to note that the average level of incidence of the uniform
tariff (48 per cent) is not appreciably higher than the average of the
previous national tariffs (42 per cent). But, reflecting the developmental orientation originally adopted, the common tariff incorporates
important changes in its internal structure.[16]

Tariff equalization is by no means a finished process in Central
America. In addition to the need for revising the uniform duties in
order to adjust them to changing conditions, the items not yet
equalized, although few in number, represent a large fraction of the
fiscal revenues derived from customs collections. However, the
solution of the latter problem lies not only in the area of tariff policy,
but much more in that of the gradual harmonization of the five
countries' fiscal systems.[17]

Free Trade under the General Treaty
of Economic Integration

By 1959, government circles in the five countries were fully aware of the need to accelerate the development of the common market. The signature of the Agreement on Tariff Equalization in that year, moreover, made it easier to reach a decision on the expansion of the free trade area. The question then was no longer whether or not there should be a forward movement in this direction, but at what speed should that movement proceed and what measures should be taken to attain it.

Two developments took place which helped to provide concrete answers to this question. One was the increasing consideration given by the governments of El Salvador and Honduras to the idea of forming a closer economic union of the two countries. The other was the newly created possibility of obtaining external co-operation to meet the financial implications of an expanded free trade area. In mid-1959 the government of the United States expressed its readiness to provide substantial co-operation, if and when the Central American countries established a complete free trade zone among themselves. A changed environment was thus created, wherein integration-minded groups and governments could develop new and more effective formulas to deal with the common market questions.

What ensued is very well known. A tripartite treaty of economic association comprising El Salvador, Honduras,and Guatemala was signed in January,1960. It was a sweeping instrument establishing immediate free trade for most goods, providing for a perfected common market in five years and creating a joint fund to finance the adjustment of productive activity to the possible unfavorable effects of free trade and to promote economic growth.[18] Various factors, mostly of a political nature, kept Nicaragua and Costa Rica out of the association at this time.

The Tripartite treaty was undeniably the breakthrough to acceler-ated progress in economic integration. But, at the same time, it undermined the geographic and political unity of the program, as well as its possibilities of survival as a wholly Central American endeavor. Restoring the program to its original membership of five countries was the purpose of intensive negotiations throughout 1960-62. The result was the General Treaty on Central American Economic Integration signed in December 1960, and the subsidiary agreements adopted since 1961.[19]

Within the framework of the common import tariff, the General Treaty provides a different solution to the question of intraregional trade, where the need to minimize disturbances in the existing systems has now given way to rapid progress in the free trade front. The procedure is actually the opposite of that adopted in the Multilateral Treaty: All goods produced in Central America are granted immediate free trade, except those included in a list subject to "temporary exceptions to free trade". This list includes products for which free trade treatment is restricted temporarily for various reasons, such as minimizing losses of fiscal revenues, providing an opportunity for certain productive activities to adjust to more competitive conditions, and allowing for the adoption of uniform duties on imports from outside the area.[20] Many of these temporary exceptions have disappeared, according to specified schedules, within a maximum period of five years ending in June, 1966.

The boldness of this solution is readily apparent. Not only was immediate free trade granted to most products--over 90 per cent of the tariff in this case--but perfecting the free trade zone was spared the tedious and undependable procedure of future negotiations, and the process was made irreversible by setting a time limit for the achievement of total free trade and by specifying in detail and in advance how this was to be accomplished.

Products comprising the larger portion of existing productive activity were initially subjected to restrictions, some of them of a rather severe nature: This is along the lines adopted in the Multilateral Treaty. However, the difference is that in the General Treaty emphasis was shifted from avoiding disturbances in the national systems, to determining ways and means to cope with those that may arise. Thus, conditions were created for what might be called "controlled disturbances," by establishing the transition period and graduating the speed at which free trade was to be reached, as well as by specifying the means to be utilized; e.g., quotas, tariff preferences, outright import-export controls, tariff equalization,or various combinations of these instruments.[21]

The problem of balanced development among countries is dealt with by the General Treaty mainly in two ways. One is through the operation of the Central American Economic Integration Bank (BCIE). This institution was given the function of channeling local and international financial resources exclusively into integration activities, and was directed to do so with a view to promoting the equitable sharing of the benefits of integration by all member countries. The other is the explicit inclusion of the 1958 Agreement on Central American Integration Industries as part of the General Treaty.[22] The status of this agreement has now been changed in the total perspective of the program. Previously, it was one way--the exceptional one--to reach free trade, together with the general procedure of the Multilateral Treaty. Now there is generalized free trade, and the application of the Integration Industries Agreement requires formal restrictions, so that, in each case, free trade will be confined to the products of particular plants and industries. Since the utilization of the agreement is optional and depends on the presentation of the corresponding applications by both governments and private entrepreneurs, it is fair to say that in this case the objective of balanced growth among countries gave way to some extent, to the objective of rapid progress in freeing trade.

Subsequent developments in 1965 and 1966, which will be analyzed in Chapter 14, have tended to bring the question of balance among countries again very much to the forefront. However, this time the problem comes up within the framework of an already established common market and not outside of it, or as a condition that might prevent its creation.

The Central American formulas for dealing with the problem of balance again differ from those adopted in other areas. For example, in the East African Common Market the solution of this problem consists mainly of the imposition of duties or quantitative restrictions to intraregional trade, so as to protect the development of certain national productions and to redress thereby industrial imbalances that have emerged over time.[23]

In the European common market emphasis has been put upon the establishment of legal conditions leading toward the maintenance of a reasonably competitive environment, to the harmonization of social charges, as well as on measures designed to equalize the benefits of economic integration by means of the free movement of labor among countries and the retraining and reorientation of occupationally displaced manpower through the operations of the European Social Fund.[24] These differences reflect in part the existence of varying degrees of commitment to the task of building a common market. But they essentially respond to different requirements of regional integration for developed countries, with advanced systems of economic organization, as compared with the countries of Central America, where industrial development is still at its initial stages.

Institutional Innovation and the Common Market

The Multilateral Free Trade Treaty was narrow in scope and slow in its procedures. Although the five countries gave themselves ten years to establish the free trade zone, they did not establish adequate mechanisms for attaining this objective. A political decision to make of the program for economic integration a genuine element of growth was lacking. Nevertheless, this Treaty was the first multinational instrument on economic policy created by the five countries. It was not a daring instrument, but then, daring decisions had all too often failed in the past. It did show the existence of common ground, painstakingly built over a period of several years and broad enough to provide sufficient room for all to stand on. This Treaty thus turned out to be the point of departure for much of what took place afterward.

To be sure, there was at the time a large measure of indecision on the part of most member governments and only lukewarm support for a real process of integration. But there were no meaningful alternatives to which they could resort. Before 1960, the possibility was lacking to institute procedures to ensure adequate accomodation of productive activities within a large and rapidly growing field of free trade. The required financial means were not available and the institutions did not exist which could dependably cope with a process of this kind.

The movement toward the rapid expansion of the Central American free trade area was helped by the fact that the embryonic stage of industrialization in the region had not given rise to powerful vested interests in the various countries. Nevertheless, it took a bit of brinkmanship to arrive at an efficient solution of the common market question. But this was certainly not the only factor in its achievement. As previously mentioned, perhaps of greater consequence were: (a) the ability of the Central American countries to formulate mechanisms and procedures designed to insert the new elements into the national systems and to cope with the difficulties that might arise, and (b) the offer of external financial assistance, which helped to remove one of the obstacles standing in the way of alternative solutions for the rapid advancement of the free trade system.

It can be argued that, given the thrust already acquired by the integration movement in 1959, the common market would soon have been a reality, with or without external aid. This is probably true, but poses a somewhat idle question. For the fact is that the above-mentioned steps were taken in the presence and not in the absence of an offer to meet their financial implications.

With respect to the procedures adopted, it is true that the search for items to be added to a list of products enjoying free trade, as in the Multilateral Treaty, was a rather sterile exercise. It was very difficult to make specific proposals on account of lack of experience and even a minimum of comparative information on markets and costs. The identification of products to be subjected to restrictions, as in the General Treaty, on the other hand, put the burden squarely on those who were in a position of finding out quickly--the private sector--and proved to be a much easier and more efficient procedure. Then the gradual approach was made meaningful by pointing out in each case the concrete means to be used and the length of the transition period. Thus, the specification of products subject to restrictions instead of those enjoying free trade, and the adoption of a time dimension to make the required adjustments came to constitute institutional inventions of far reaching importance.

Footnotes to Chapter 8

1. For the initial resolutions see United Nations, Report of the Economic Commission for Latin America, Fourth Session (E/2021) (New York, 1951), p. 20.

2. For the texts of these and other economic agreements of Central American scope, see United Nations, Economic Commission for Latin America, Convenios Centroamericanos de Integración Económica (E/CN.12/CCE/315) (Mexico City, 1964), /mimeographed/.

3. Banco Centroamericano de Integración Económica, Primera Memoria de Labores, 1961, 1962 (Tegucigalpa, 1962), pp. 45-6.

4. Specific references to the various technical documents and governmental decisions are included in the Bibliography, at the end of this study.

5. See United Nations, Economic Commission for Latin America, Documentación del Comité de Cooperación Económica del Istmo Centroamericano (CEPAL/MEX/65/5) (Mexico City, 1965), /mimeographed/.

6. United Nations, Nomenclatura Arancelaria Uniforme Centroamericana (NAUCA) y su Manual de Codificación, (E/CN.12/420) (New York, 1955).

7. Multilateral Free Trade Treaty, Articles I to VI.

8. Montevideo Treaty, Articles 1, 2 and 3.

9. Montevideo Treaty, Articles 4 through 8.

10. Montevideo Treaty, Article 32.

11. Agreement on the Regime of Central American Integration Industries, Articles II, III and IV; a more detailed analysis of this Agreement is made in Chapter 13 below.

12. For a more detailed account of the methods used, see United Nations, Economic Commission for Latin America, Informe de la Duodécima Reunión del Subcomité de Comercio Centroamericano, (E/CN.12/CCE/247) (Mexico City, 1962), pp. 1-5, /mimeographed/.

13. Agreement on Tariff Equalization, Article II and Schedule B.

14. See East Africa, Report of the Economic and Fiscal Commission (London: Her Majesty's Stationery Office, (Cmnd. 1279), 1961), p. 7.

15. Treaty of Rome, Article 19.

16. From unpublished data prepared by the United Nations, Economic Commission for Latin America (Mexico City, 1963).

17. United Nations, Economic Commission for Latin America, Evaluación de la Integración Económica Centroamericana, op. cit., p. 60.

18. Banco Nacional de Comercio Exterior, S. A., La Integración Económica Latinoamericana (Mexico City, 1963), pp. 927-33.

19. United Nations, Economic Commission for Latin America, Report of the Central American Economic Co-operation Committee, Seventh Session, (E/CN.12/552) (Mexico City, June 1961), pp. 13-47.

20. General Treaty, Articles III-IV and Annex A.

21. General Treaty, Annex A.

22. General Treaty, Articles XVII and XVIII, and Agreement establishing the Central American Bank for Economic Integration, Article 2.

23. See Nils Ramm-Ericson, Restrictions Affecting the Interterritorial Trade between Kenya, Tanzania and Uganda. A memorandum prepared for the Economic Division of the Treasury, East African Common Services Organization (EACSO) (Nairobi, 1966), /mimeographed/.

24. Treaty of Rome, Articles 48-51, 85-94 and 117-28.

CHAPTER **9** THE PROGRAM
AND THE
ECONOMY

Intraregional Trade and Investment

During the first few years, there was hardly any relationship
between the program for economic integration and the actual workings
of the economy. The main actions were still on the drawing boards of
policy makers, while the bilateral trade treaties were narrow in scope
and did not have the breadth and sweep of a truly multilateral instrument. This is why it could be asserted in 1961, on signing the General
Treaty, that all was well with the economic integration program, but
that much was not well with the performance of the economy. Five
years later the relationship is still weak: The traditional export sector
is still--by far--the main determinant of economic activity in the
region, and not enough time has elapsed for the common market to
develop fully, while much of the productive structure continues to
operate within the limits of national demands.

The weakness diminishes as time passes and the volume of trade
among the five countries is no longer negligible. It stood at about
8 million dollars in 1952, when imports from all sources amounted to
little over 200 million dollars. By 1965, imports from Central American
countries had increased more than seventeen times, to over 140 million
dollars, with imports from all sources somewhat lower than 900 million
dollars. The share of intraregional imports thus rose fourfold over the
thirteen year period, from 4 to 16 per cent. [1]

Qualitative changes have also taken place in the commercial
relationships among the five countries. At the beginning, intraregional
trade was regarded in some countries as a way out of occasional
surpluses or shortages of agricultural products. This did not make for

a trade movement organized around permanent flows of goods, resulting, therefore, in an inherently unstable situation. Between 1950 and 1955 the value of intra-Central American imports of farm products grew at 18.1 per cent per annum, while that of manufactured goods increased only at 1.4 per cent. The pattern changed after 1955, as production for export to the rest of Central America began to be viewed as a normal operation. Intraregional trade started to grow at much higher rates and its composition changed in favor of manufactured products. Thus, between 1955 and 1960, the total value of intraregional imports increased at an annual rate of 20 per cent, as against 9 per cent during the previous five year period; imports of farm products increased 12.0 per cent yearly, while those of manufactures rose at an impressive yearly rate of 26 per cent. These trends have been further intensified in 1960-65, when total intraregional trade expanded at an annual rate of 34 per cent.[2]

It must be pointed out that the stepped up pace of 1955-60 occurred at a time when the terms of trade fell by 24.2 per cent.[3] After 1960, when the traditional export sector recovered on account of improved price conditions and of substantial increments in the volume of exports, intraregional trade continued to grow at higher rates than in previous years.

The expansion of intraregional trade must reflect a substantial increase in industrial investment induced by the common market over the past decade. But the available data is extremely scanty. It is known that in El Salvador, for example, new productive capacity was designed and competitive conditions evaluated in terms of a regional, rather than a purely national, operation even before the common market was established. In addition, figures gathered recently indicate that private investment conceived entirely with a view to supplying the common market--including plants already in existence and projects under way--amounted to about 100 million dollars during 1961-65.[4]

Investment in public works programs is also beginning to be influenced by the common market; schemes for a regional road network, interconnection of national electric power systems between pairs of countries, telecommunications, and storage facilities for agricultural products--all of which are also at varying stages of development --already reach well beyond the 300 million dollar mark.[5] Some idea of the relative magnitude of these figures can be obtained by comparing them with the total annual investment--public and private--for the region as a whole, which amounted to about 150 million dollars during the late 1950's.[6]

The Combined Effect of Free Trade and
Tariff Equalization

Behind these trends of intraregional trade and investments is the fact that, in establishing a free trade area and in erecting a common tariff, these countries have altered the extent and the workings of their internal markets or, more precisely, of the markets which are available to internal production. The initial impact has been to enlarge each of the national markets by an average factor of at least 5. This has been done either by granting immediate free trade to Central American goods or by establishing, through firm commitments, the expectation of its attainment over a maximum period of five years.

Widening the extent of the available market and increasing internal production are two different things. If existing productive capacity is fully utilized, the enlargement of the market will induce new investments in plant and equipment; and several years may elapse before appreciable increases in production and trade take place. But if there is unemployment and idle capacity, the expanded market provides an opportunity for its utilization, thus resulting in short-run increases of output. This is what happened in Central America. Lower prices in the international markets led to substantial unemployment and underutilization of physical plant throughout the regional economy,beginning in 1955.

The expansion of the free trade area together with the effects of the uniform tariff facilitated the utilization of part of that idle capacity and unemployed manpower, especially in the manufacturing sector, thus enabling the economy to withstand better the consequences of the crisis. By doing this in terms of a multinational expansion of the market for internal production, it provided at the same time the first real thrust to Central American economic integration. In this way, a portion of the internal economy was reclaimed from its traditional immediate dependence on the external sector and put to work as the source of the very rapid growth experienced by intraregional trade since 1955.

Idle resources and productive capacity seem to have been present whenever there has been need for major economic adjustments in Central America. Such was the case when Independence was achieved and the direction of foreign trade radically altered; it was also the situation when the export economy began to be developed, and again

when the common market was launched. This is at variance with the
assumption of full employment generally made in the theoretical
literature on customs unions. Such an assumption is made in order to
simplify the analysis, so as to avoid having to trace the evolution of
a given system to the point where it is fully utilizing its existing
capacity. But it can lead to error on two counts. In the first place,
it is difficult to find the need for radical socioeconomic changes under
conditions of full employment. In the second place, utilization of idle
capacity may provide the basis not to stabilize an existing pattern but
to begin to change it, either by altering the composition of production,
the markets where it is sold, or both.

The relationship between integration and the economy begins to
gain strength also as the common market starts to influence not only the
degree of utilization but also the size and structure of productive
capacity, through its effects upon the volume and the composition of
new investment. As noted in Chapter 5, several factors contributed to
the orientation of some investment toward the internal market in the
Central American countries since the early 1940's. In addition to the
experiences of the war period with the first attempts to replace certain
imports with local production, falling prices of exports and rising
national tariffs subsequently influenced the structure of relative prices
so as to make that type of investment more attractive. The common
market reinforced these trends by providing larger outlets to investment
funds which did not find adequate opportunities in the export economy.
In this way, free trade and tariff policy--through bilateralism and the
expectation of the common market--provided a focus and a wider avenue
for developments which had begun to occur during World War II, such
as establishment of manufactures, electric power development, road
construction to better structure the internal economy,and the building
of the Inter-American Highway.

Other sectors of the economy have begun to expand under the
impulse of the common market. Intraregional trade and investment
have given rise to increased volumes of credit and to the creation of
private investment companies, in addition to the Central American
Economic Integration Bank. Transport services are expanding to meet
regional needs. They serve the rapidly growing passenger traffic
within the region as well as between Central America and Mexico and
Panama; they also move sizable volumes of freight among the common
market countries. Finally, insurance and technical services of
regional scope are beginning to be established.

The Common Market and the Traditional Economy

Although traditional exports still dominate the Central American economies, some structural relationships are already undergoing appreciable changes. This refers to relationships within the monetized sector of the economy as well as between this sector and the rest of the system. Each country, each productive activity, and each firm are facing two new facts in varying degrees: One is the opportunity to provide employment for more of their resources, to produce at higher levels of output and to increase their sales; the other is their exposure to a more keenly competitive environment.

The first elements of the modern function of entrepreneurship can be observed, where in the past there was only the routine operation of an unchanging agricultural export economy. The new entrepreneurs are already realizing some of the opportunities created by the common market. They have increased the output of existing plants and have invested in their expansion. They are hard at work in the establishment of market connections and allied services and are beginning to operate with an eye on the behavior of their Central American competitors. These are some of the factors influencing the workings of the monetized economy in its internal relationships.

The creation of the common market has also affected relationships between the export sector and the international markets. A sustained increase in foreign exchange earnings, say as a result of several years of improved prices in the international markets, can now have a greater influence than before upon the strength of internal demand and the volume of domestic investment. By the same token, a fall in foreign exchange earnings would tend to depress internal activity more than it did under the previous system. This is so because the regional economy is becoming increasingly dependent on imported investment and production inputs. As these are reduced, as a result of decline in foreign income, they affect directly the level of internal production.

In addition, the monetary and foreign exchange policies of the five countries are now reciprocally influenced in two ways: First, the actions of any member country in this field may be reinforced or counteracted by those of its partners; second, these policies must differentiate between the other members of the common market and the rest of the world. The probability of problems arising on the first count with respect to economic integration is not high, at least for the immediate future. The economies operate under the influence of the same basic factors,and their governments, working with the International Monetary Fund, follow the same lines of policy in relation to the quantity of money, the volume of credit,and the level of public expenditures.

It is on the second count that difficulties may arise for the common market in the years immediately ahead. Article VIII of the Multilateral Treaty and Article X of the General Treaty call on the central banks to co-operate with a view to maintaining the convertibility of the five national currencies. They provide that such restrictions that may be established on international currency transfers by any of the countries should not discriminate against other Central American countries and that, in case of serious balance-of-payment difficulties, measures will be taken to preserve the unimpeded functioning of the multilateral free trade system.

Between 1961 and 1966 there was no cause for concern over the application of these clauses, since foreign exchange earnings have been rising, as a result of the partial recovery of prices and the increased volume of regional exports. But problems of excess supply and lower prices in the international markets may emerge once more, particularly in the case of coffee, which is still the main source of foreign exchange in the area. Consequently, the harmonization of the national monetary and foreign exchange policies and the establishment of adequate mechanisms for this purpose are among the most urgent tasks of the integration program. Important steps have been taken in this direction through the creation of the Central American Clearing House and periodic consultations among the central banks. However, much remains to be done in order to ensure that the functioning of the common market is not disturbed by unilateral actions arising from balance-of-payments difficulties.

As suggested in Chapter 7, the common market will tend to establish larger demands for food upon subsistence agriculture, by inducing higher rates of growth in the monetized sector of the economy. So far agriculture has performed reasonably well; but so far the Central American economies have been growing slowly. If their rate of growth is to be increased and kept at higher levels, total output of domestic agriculture and the fraction thereof entering commercial channels will have to keep pace with the rest of the economy and under conditions of improved quality and lower costs. Only thus will it be possible to further strengthen internal demand in Central America.[7]

To be sure, these are problems not of economic integration, but of economic development, whether national or multinational. What is now directly related to economic integration is the framework for their solution. Intraregional trade has already made it possible for Central America to become self-sufficient in food staples by permitting it to balance out localized situations of surpluses and shortages. But in addition to the advantage of more fluid movements of farm products, the common market has made it possible for domestic agriculture to develop under conditions of a much higher degree of geographic specialization, following more closely the lines of resource capabilities. It has also established a base upon which greater efforts can be made by bringing together into a regional action some of the physical, technical, financial, and organizational resources available at the national level, and by promoting a better distribution of the Central American population relative to the resources at their disposal.

The Need for a Regional Policy of Common Market Development

Although the accomplishments to date are impressive, there is still a long way to go in the task of structuring the future pattern of growth in Central America. The common market is largely completed in its legal texts, but in actual practice it is still building. Free trade and tariff equalization are only gradually reaching the required degree of dependability with respect to both their permanence over time and their application to specific transactions. The commercial sector is just beginning to turn toward Central American products, and the necessary network of market connections for intraregional trade is still in a rudimentary stage.

Furthermore, trade within the common market can grow on the basis of fuller utilization of existing productive plants only up to a point. Obviously, additional capacity will be needed. Expansion of this capacity in the form of the undersized plants and obsolete equipment, of the type which often had to be built for the national market in the past, would keep costs at high levels. New investment in existing productive activities may lead into problems of duplication and idle resources.

The very high rates of growth experienced by intraregional trade since 1955 depict a process similar in kind to that which stimulated the rise of Central America's exports and imports during the 1820's, when a liberal trade policy resulted immediately in substantial gains through utilization of available resources. But, as will be recalled, that was a short-lived phenomenon. Similarly, the rapid expansion of recent years can come to an end, if it continues to be based only on the present productive structure. Unless a drastic redistribution of income were to take place in favor of the economically weaker groups, which seems unlikely at this juncture, a static structure of this type would soon find definite limitations in its high import requirements, slow-growing demands, and diminishing possibilities for further import substitution.

As these processes begin to unfold in actual practice, they reveal that the common market has to develop much stronger roots. There is not as yet any real interdependence among the Central American economies and their behavior is only starting to adjust to the newly acquired dimensions.

Therefore, the issue is how to strengthen the multinational effort, what to build, and how to build on the foundations laid thus far. And the issue is joined in the development of a productive structure commensurate with the size of the regional unit, in exploiting the productive opportunities that have been created with the consolidation of the five national markets. This will take time, but it will not be achieved simply with the passage of time and only on the basis of the measures already taken. What is done to develop a productive structure of the kind that will make of the common market the starting point for Central America's future growth is the central problem of the program for economic integration as it enters its third phase.

In establishing free trade and a uniform tariff, the member countries have altered the internal economy only on the demand side. The productive structure remains largely the same. Changing it will take time in any event, but it should be stressed that what has been done so far cannot, in and of itself, change the capabilities of the internal economy. It seems that in the proportioning of elements which make up the economic going concern, there is a direct relationship between the size and number of available opportunities and the nature and strength of the system's capabilities. So that, when the Central American common market was created, the potentialities of the productive systems, taken separately, continued to correspond to those of the pre-existing national markets.

This is why the typical Central American businessman continues to invest in the same economic activities, undersized plants and obsolete industrial processes. That is what he knows. To him regional free trade is only an opportunity to do a little more of the same. In so doing, he is not conducting himself irrationally; he is doing what he can with the elements at his disposal.

It also explains why the type of productive ventures that are the distinctively new elements contributed by the program are being promoted by foreign interests almost without exception (fertilizers, oil refining, tires, insecticides, electric bulbs, etc.) and why some of the local industrialists are beginning to sell out to outside interests when the need arises to enlarge and modernize the plants they have erected. For the Central American entrepreneur lacks the organizational skills, technology, financing and, of course, the experience which foreign enterprises have. The possibilities created through economic integration do not include these things; they are governed by other processes. The creation of meaningful opportunities for their acquisition must be one of the principal elements in any common market development policy.

A century ago the internal production of these countries was nearly obliterated by imports from the industrial areas and by the newly established export lines. Internal industrial activities are again running into a similar situation, though in different circumstances. They find themselves unable to reorganize and to compete with the larger, more modern and efficient plants that are beginning to be established. There is the question as to whether or not the now small managerial class will grow in these countries as opportunities arise to carry out the new productive possibilities.

It is in this kind of economic experience that the need for a regional policy finds its historical roots. Many requirements will have to be fulfilled. Ways and means must be found to channel internal resources toward new possibilities; investment will have to be based upon new forms of organization where family control gives way to co-operation among groups from various member countries; close contacts and various forms of association will have to be worked out with foreign interests, not only for financial purposes but also for the establishment of access to valuable experiences, techniques, and market connections, and vigorous programs must be implemented to provide for a continuous flow of scientific and technological knowledge into Central America, as well as for its adaptation to the conditions prevailing in the region.

The region's future growth may depend to a large extent on the actions that are taken now with respect to the development of the productive structure. It must not be overlooked that the immediate growth possibilities offered by the common market are relatively not very large, certainly not as large as those which the international market provided one hundred years ago.[8] Taking advantage of these opportunities will contribute to Central America's development and result in a substantial enlargement of its productive capacity. But carrying them out as they come, along the lines of the existing pattern, without selectivity and, most important, without an overall purpose for the future, would soon exhaust this initial push. The traditional export sector would then continue to dictate the rate of economic development, determining the evolution of internal demand and now the availability of imported inputs as well.

Alternatively, a policy of common market development could speed up the identification of new productive opportunities and promote their implementation in such a way as to gain for Central America additional impetus for economic growth. This will require the construction of a productive structure operating at decreasing costs and increasing productivity. Achieving this objective and transforming the gains so obtained into a larger market, by means of their widespread distribution among the population, will add new impulses to the enlargement of economic activity. The extent to which this is accomplished will determine in no small measure (a) the amount of sustained development that will take place; (b) the ease and success with which Central America will be able to participate in the international economy; (c) the degree to which the economy will belong to Central Americans, and (d) how the benefits and burdens of economic integration will be shared by the member countries.

It is now clear that, important as it is, what has been done so far in the field of Central American integration amounts to having bought an opportunity to build the region's economic development. The opportunity is here; the development is in the future. This is the challenge.

Footnotes to Chapter 9

1. Based on data published by the Permanent Secretariat of the General Treaty (SIECA) in: Tercer Compendio Estadístico Centroamericano (Guatemala City, 1963), Table L-21; and in the statistical supplements to its Carta Mensual (Monthly Letter) published since that date.

2. Idem; see also, United Nations, Economic Commission for Latin America, La Economía de América Latina en 1965 (Santiago, Chile, 1966), p. 27.

3. United Nations, Economic Commission for Latin America, El sector externo y el desarrollo económico de Centroamérica, 1950-62, (CCE/SC.I/R.Ex.I/DI.2) (Mexico City, January 1964), p. 9.

4. United Nations, Economic Commission for Latin America, from data furnished by the Permanent Secretariat of the General Treaty.

5. See above, Chapter 7, footnote 6.

6. United Nations, Economic Commission for Latin America, from official government statistics.

7. For analyses of the general issues involved, see Walt W. Rostow, "Agriculture's role in economic development," Foreign Agriculture, Vol. I, No. 35, USDA (Washington, September 1963), and Carlos M. Castillo, "La agricultura tradicional en una economía en desarrollo," El Trimestre Económico, Vol. XXX (4) No. 120 (Mexico City: Fondo de Cultura Económica, October-December 1963), pp. 659-68.

8. United Nations, Economic Commission for Latin America, "Los problemas de la política industrial centroamericana," Boletín Económico de América Latina, Vol. IX, No. 1 (Santiago, Chile, March 1964), pp. 120-21 and 123.

CHAPTER **10** THE CONSTRUCTION
OF A REGIONAL
APPROACH

The Common Market and the Economy:
A Growing Interdependence

Without sustained growth, economic integration could make it
more difficult at this stage for each country to cope with problems of
balance of payments, foreign exchange, fiscal revenues and industrial
development. This is so because the common market has reduced the
scope of national action in the fields of trade, monetary and tax
policies, as well as in tax concessions for the promotion of new
industries.[1] By the same token, the continued expansion of the
economy will contribute by making it easier to effect the adjustments
of groups and industries that are called for.

Sustained economic growth will not follow automatically upon the
establishment of the common market, but as closer economic links are
established among the five countries, it will become increasingly difficult to separate the problems of development from those of integration.
For they arise out of the same process which in the long run will tend
to change the common market into the core of Central American
growth. This is a large task, and its complexities are just beginning
to be grasped. Much remains to be known about it in the Central
American setting. Experiences elsewhere are few and difficult to
translate into terms that are meaningful for the problems at hand.
Therefore, it is all the more important, when dealing with these
problems, to keep in sight the main lessons of the region's economic
history and to rely on methods of attack that have proved to be
dependable in arriving at adequate solutions.

The lessons of history, going back to the nineteenth century,
suggest that the new elements to be added to the system should be so
utilized as to make it possible, through appropriate adjustments, for
these countries to consolidate and strengthen the economic gains they

have achieved to date, rather than allowing them to destroy what has taken a long time and much hard work to build. They point out the need to turn the new elements to advantage in propagating the process of growth throughout the economy, instead of confining them to only some sectors of activity.

The lessons of history also call for a large measure of care in the ways in which the advancement of economic integration is promoted. Looking back at the efforts to reconstruct the regional union between 1840 and 1921, it is important to avoid in the present the hurried, oversimplified approach, which makes for headlines today but results in failure tomorrow. It is also important, probably more so than before, not to overlook that progress in economic integration can only be based upon strong elements of national support in the member countries and not upon supplanting these elements with self-appointed regional institutions of whatever kind they may be. In the end these are likely to prove rootless, powerless, and wasteful of time and resources.

To be sure, historical ties have been an important factor conducive to the formation of the common market. But this should not close our eyes to the present political situation in the region. The identification that may have been observed in the five countries with a Central American entity in the early years of their political independence has given way to strong elements of five national points of view and, what is more important, to more effective means to ensure that these elements carry their weight. There is also the apparent paradox that although the common market has increased the relationships of interdependence, at the same time it has provided a frame of reference against which national points of view can be sharpened and subjected to constant comparison.

Methods Making for the Success of Economic
Integration to Date

The dependable methods to be used in coping with the problems of integration also grow out of historical experience, this time going back to the first stages of the program over the last decade. Admittedly, it is a short period for a definitive evaluation, but the fact that this program has succeeded so far, where past efforts had failed, suggests that the methods making for its success should be studied with a view to determining their possible usefulness in the solution of present and future problems.

In so doing it must be kept in mind that these methods have not
operated in a vacuum, but have rather developed in an environment
where some of the elements have been conducive to economic integration. Within this framework, the strategic elements in the success
of the program for economic integration are two: The way in which the
Central American countries have organized themselves to formulate,
test, adopt, and implement integration measures; and the type of
changes which these measures have sought to effect vis-à-vis the
national economies.

As for the first element, the institution of a thorough process of
investigation as a basis for governmental action at the regional level
has been most important. Several aspects stand out in the process.
One is the development of basic studies on the issues to which action
is to be applied. Another is the free examination and discussion of
these studies jointly by government officials of the member countries
at various levels (technical, executive, political), for the purpose of
preparing the blueprints for concrete measures; this has provided a vital
interaction between the research effort and those in need of its results.

Taking advantage of more localized experiences, such as bilateral
trade treaties and national legislation for industrial development, has
also been important in the formulation of action toward integration.
This has facilitated the development of Central American legislation,
and has made it possible also to introduce substantial improvements in
the contents of policy as well as to sharpen some of its objectives, as
illustrated in the uniform tariff on imports and in the uniform tax incentives to industrial growth. In the case of the uniform tariff, specific
development criteria were added to traditional fiscal and balance-of-
payments considerations, in order to promote industrialization and
import substitution. With regard to fiscal incentives, the Central
American Agreement provides that tax exemption will be so utilized
as to foster the establishment of an industrial structure based upon
strong reinforcing relationships among productive activities and the
fullest possible utilization of the region's resources.

As for the second element, having to do with the kind of changes
that it has been sought to effect, the program for economic integration
has succeeded because, in addition to their intrinsic efficacy, the
measures it has formulated have been viable measures. And they have
been viable because in their immediate purposes they have attempted to
add new dimensions to the going concerns of the national economies,
instead of to supplant existing opportunities; they have also softened
the effects of regional action upon economic activity at the national

level by means of adjustment periods and specification of the ways in which such effects will be allowed to take place.

At the same time, in their workings and in their sequence the regional agreements have provided effective means to accommodate the varying major interests of the member countries. One reason why this was possible was that, on closer examination, it was found in most instances that the apparently national interests of one country coincided with those of the other member countries, thus reflecting a general problem of the region as a whole. This was true, for example, with respect to El Salvador's insistence on widespread free trade, Costa Rica's preoccupation on tariff equalization, and Nicaragua's case for regional integration industries. Save for the issue of balanced growth among countries, which to this date remains one of the crucial unsettled questions, it has been possible in this way to provide reasonably satisfactory solutions to the major problems faced by economic integration in Central America. This has permitted the program to proceed with the continuing support and willing participation of the five member countries, and to remain outside the factional, partisan struggles of national and regional politics.

Changing Nature of the Program
in the Third Phase

The methods that have made for a successful integration program will continue to perform a useful role in achieving success in the future. However, emphasis will change as new problems arise. The present third phase differs from the previous ones, in which treaty making was the main task before the governments. From now on, the program must increasingly take on the not so glamorous task of making treaties and institutions work. This entails building, securing, and reinforcing at the points where the newly established working rules so far have created only an opportunity still small and perhaps weak, and of making sure--through perfecting and consolidating actions--that in time what are now legal texts evolve toward more formal expressions of a sturdier reality.

There is another difference. Previously the objective was to establish a framework, a scaffolding, wherein economic integration could take place; the aim now is to build inside that scaffolding, to devise a policy for growth within that framework. In the third phase, the

question is, therefore, how to realize the possibilities and opportunities that have been created; in other words, how to use the instruments already established, in order to transform their intended purpose
into actual developments.

Thus, there are differences between the present and the previous
phases of the program. But there is also a common denominator
bringing them together as part of a single process. Now, as before,
the issues of policy hinge on the question of what actions should be
taken, and what instruments should be established for the purpose of
enlarging economic opportunity through integration. The creation of
the common market consisted of a modification in the existing working
rules; through free trade Central American goods were segregated from
the general category of imported goods and accorded preferential
treatment--the norms applying to national goods--while the operations
of national action were aggregated by means of tariff equalization, so
as to apply uniformly throughout the common market to all goods imported from outside Central America.

So there is no change here as to the kind of questions to which
public policy will have to address itself in the field of economic integration. If anything, there will be now a greater need to develop a
larger number of increasingly complex norms. In general, the. functions
and even the presence of these working rules are not so apparent in traditional, stagnant economies, since everything is known and proceeds
without disturbance, as if guided by an invisible hand. But when change
begins to take place, which is the very essence of growth, their
existence and their need are more readily felt, as it becomes indispensable to modify them and to define new ones.[2] Treaty administration and formulation of a growth policy within the common market
are the sources of that greater need and provide the directions for their
development in the present phase of the program.

The elimination of existing restrictions within the common market
will make it necessary for previously established economic activities
to adjust to the conditions of free trade. This is precisely the purpose
behind the decision to create the transition period of five years. And
this adjustment calls in many cases for the development of new legislation of Central American scope regarding such matters as commercial
policy, tariff equalization,and coordination of marketing programs.
Managing the common market will give rise to other requirements as it
will have to address itself increasingly to adjudicate emerging conflicts
and to provide adequate responses to new demands. Additional norms
will be needed to cope with situations having to do with changes in the

uniform external tariff, harm inflicted by free trade on existing activities, and legitimate and non-ligitimate taxation on Central
American goods. They will also have to expand into new fields and
tackle, for example, the problems arising from unfair competition and
business practices in restraint of trade.[3]

The need to solve these questions is now greater than before. Prior
to the establishment of the common market, the problems facing the
integration program had no direct effects upon ongoing productive activities; now they cost money and, depending on how they are dealt
with, the actions to which they give rise will affect the revenues of
the State, the profits of some business firms, the survival of others, or
the welfare of consumers.

Policy questions regarding development within the common market
loom large in this context. New procedures will be needed to enlarge
the going concern of economic integration so as to gear the operations
of the national systems and the functioning of national institutions to
the conditions created by the common market; to protect and stimulate
Central American enterprises, to modify the structure and conditions
of the credit systems and to organize intergovernmental action in
fields other than intraregional trade and the tariffs. More specifically,
those questions call for, among other things, the completion of a
regional policy of industrial development, the harmonization of national fiscal systems and the formulation of a Central American commercial
policy vis-à-vis the rest of the world.[4]

All of these developments will take place gradually, as the five
economies become increasingly interdependent, productive activity
grows and diversifies, new groups emerge in the structure of economic
power, and the governments change as participants and moulders of this
structure. Growing out of all of these processes, a far reaching legal
reform will take place, consisting not only of an increase in legis -
lative, executive, and customary norms, but also of qualitative changes
in the new, relative to existing, legislation. Although radically
different in its scope and substantive contents, it will be similar in
kind to the legal reform that was effected during the second half of the
nineteenth century so as to make room for Central America's first stage
of economic development.

Several categories may be differentiated. Rules will be needed
for the specific and detailed implementation of free trade and tariff
equalization; these will be embodied in the executive development of
the General Treaty and other basic legal instruments. Others will be

required to facilitate the operation of the common market; they will give rise to uniform statutes on commercial law, customs administration, banking legislation, and transportation. Still others will have to be worked out to provide for adequate accommodation between industries and economic interests; they will consist of regional agreements for the regulation of monopoly power, unfair competition, and restraints of trade. Together they will constitute the framework defining the limits, the rights, duties, liberties, and exposures, [5] according to which economic integration is to proceed.

A new element will run throughout these developments, namely that all of them will belong in the category of international law; they will govern a growing system of economic relationships among five countries, relating to the operations of the private economy as well as to actions among governments. Moreover, although some of them will be substantively similar to existing statutes, quite a few will be qualitatively different. These belong to the category of administrative and regulatory law which, by the very nature of its subject matter, cannot provide specific substantive solutions to all the problems that may arise, but relies rather on procedural operations designed to establish the various cases and then to seek appropriate solutions.

In this respect administrative and regulatory law differs from that which now characterizes the Central American legal systems. Substantively, the latter provide specific solutions for specific cases, while procedurally, their operations are designed to implement these solutions rather than to construct them with the materials conforming the various cases. The experiences of the industrialized countries show that regulation and administration become increasingly important as an economic system begins to develop under conditions of a diversifying productive structure. Although, for obvious reasons, administrative and regulatory law has achieved only modest gains in Central America, it is not unknown in these countries, as exemplified by the existing electric power and other public utility commissions.

Methods for the Expansion of Economic Integration

No one can foretell the substance of all the measures that will be required nor anticipate their sequence in time; for they encompass an extremely wide field of activities and situations in a process that reaches far out into the future.

Nevertheless, it is possible to devise procedures and mechanisms that will be useful in anticipating these situations as much as possible and that will help to settle the corresponding issues as they emerge. It is at this juncture that the methods used successfully in the program for economic integration become applicable again.

The thorough investigation of problems as they come up before action is formulated and taken for their solution, has been efficacious on repeated occasions. Within this process, the development of research and the free discussion and confrontation of its results jointly by responsible officials of the member governments will continue to perform an important role. In fact, in some cases it may be necessary to formalize these operations and to spell them out in detail as legal requirements, so as to provide for certainty in change, dependability in the procedures and efficacy in the accommodation of the various interests involved.[6]

Taking advantage of more localized experiences will continue to provide useful elements in the formulation of measures of regional scope to further the advancement of economic integration. This should be not only allowed but also promoted in all fields where it will not interfere with the operation of the established multilateral schemes and where circumstances are still not ripe for action at the Central American level. Functioning unimpeded within this sphere of discretion for institutional innovation, the action of the various countries ought to contribute in fields such as interconnection of electric power systems, coordination of national programs on regional highways,and joint administration of price support programs for farm products.[7]

The actual performance of the common market will also give rise to new requirements opening up additional areas for joint action. This is the case, for example, of the already felt needs for coordinating the fiscal systems, regulating the assembly industries,and providing measures to put the Central American entrepreneurial groups on a more equal footing with respect to their foreign competitors. In this way, improvement in the functioning of the common market and progress in economic integration will often grow in the future as the unobtrusive, seemingly natural result of the workings of processes already operating throughout the Central American economies.

Looking at these issues from the vantage point of the region's economic history, it soon becomes clear that generalizing from more localized experiences and enlarging the going concern of economic integration at the growing points of the common market provide the

way to propagate the processes of development throughout the system.
Politically this could be less difficult to attain than the previous
achievements of the program. The establishment of the common market
took a fairly big decision that had to be based largely on expectations.
It amounted, as it were, to the taking of a new road, one which had
not been traveled before. Now the political decisions are smaller in
scope, thus less difficult to take, and they can be based upon performance. They are not a choice at crossroads, but actions as to how
and how fast the journey is to take place along the chosen path.

Due Process of Policy

Research studies, joint examination of their results and pragmatic
experience will make it possible to establish a sort of due process for
the development of economic integration in the future. Its need is
here and will grow, as it becomes more and more apparent that this
development will take place only on the basis of the efficient operation of existing schemes. This means that reorganizations, reforms,
additions, juggling and rejuggling of the treaties and other Central
American institutions must not be allowed to occur capriciously, as
soon as, and whenever something seems to start going wrong with them.
They must be treated, rather, with the greatest care and respect; their
positive achievements must be protected at all costs, and their new
elements given a chance to work.[8] To restrict the possibility for
ample experimentation is to take away from the program its main
source of strength; for partial failures and imperfections are likely to
occur in any human endeavor. It must be kept in mind that the program
for economic integration has been the only effort that has brought the
Central Americans together, in more than one century. If it is to stay,
to take root and grow, different means will have to be used than those
attempted in previous efforts to reconstruct the Central American
Union.

On the basis of the methods used to date in the program, a due
process for the development of economic integration should be
structured around four operations designed to determine (a) the purpose
of proposed action, (b) its efficiency as a means to achieve the intended objectives, (c) its adaptation to available capabilities and
(d) its insertion into the ongoing systems of national, regional and
international Central American relationships.

The determination of purpose aims at clarifying whether or not
proposed action belongs legitimately to the field of economic

integration. The legitimacy of purpose requires much more than the good omen of getting together in meetings. It is important that this be realized, in order to be able to select, from the numerous proposals that are being made ever since the common market came into being, the few that are good, as against the many that are merely interesting or preposterous.

An additional criterion to be kept in mind is that further growth is achieved by building upon what has been done successfully, not by adding haphazardly all over. This has made for a certain logic in the sequence followed so far in the development of the program   and now takes on greater importance. For, while in the beginning it may have been possible to be less concerned about the outcome of particular decisions, this is no longer the case with the common market operating as a functioning enterprise.

On the other hand, there are many issues of public policy which can and must be dealt with at the national level. It follows, therefore, that the framework of economic integration is not useful for each and everything. Especially, it should not be used to postpone measures that each country has to adopt in order to put its own house in order in the field of wealth and income distribution. In other words, economic integration is not a way to evade reforms by exporting the problems to the rest of the region. A regional approach may facilitate some of these changes, in fields such as agrarian reform, social insurance, wage policy and fiscal reform, but it is certainly no substitute for them.

Once the issue of large or ultimate objectives is settled, as has been in the case of Central American economic integration, the problem of the efficiency of the means to be used becomes paramount. This problem can be handled by breaking down the larger targets into smaller objectives set up in such a way that they lend themselves to the application of public action, and by making certain that this action will lead to the attainment of the ends in view. There are many ex- amples of past national or regional efforts in which this procedure was not adopted. The attempt to establish the "República Mayor Centro- americana" in 1898, is perhaps an extreme one, though not atypical. The basic agreements of the "República" defined only large objectives which, of necessity, had to be vague; they did not break down these objectives at all and failed to provide the means, any means, for their implementation. As for the adequacy of instruments to reach stated objectives, the annals of the Central American countries abound in executive orders and legislative contracts providing monopoly powers, tax exemptions, and land grants as rewards for technological

inventions, organization of commercial banks, establishment of manufacturing industries, and construction of railroads and waterways which
never materialized.[9]

Another aspect of the question of efficiency, defined here as a
separate operation, is that of the relationship between proposed action
and available capabilities. Taking account of this relationship immediately eliminates theoretical possibilities as premature. One of
these, for example, is the immediate abolition of customs at the
borders between member countries. This would make for a smoother
flow of goods within the region, but it would also raise serious fiscal
and administrative problems which the governments are not prepared to
handle at this time. As for the more real possibilities, the problem
subsists of adequately gearing action to capabilities. This implies
choosing actions that can be taken with the resources at hand, and
providing simultaneously for the development of the capabilities that
may be lacking, timing the implementation of decisions accordingly.
Thus, for example, it will not be possible for several years to base
industrial development policies upon actions requiring a highly skilled
public administration. Executives and technicians must begin to be
trained and formed now and the timing of such actions adjusted to the
rate of their development.

Within the context of objectives, means, and alternatives into
which matters of economic integration issue in Central America, the
question of the consequences of proposed action upon the workings of
the national economy looms large in the minds of responsible government officials. At least the main consequences must be clarified in
advance if action is to survive at the regional level. Obviously, this
usually gives rise to the need for compromise, so as to establish an
adequate relationship with other parts of the national systems. From
now on, such a process will have to be extended to the clarification of
the consequences following upon the functioning of the common market
and upon Central America's relationships with the rest of the world. To
illustrate with current issues: One of the reasons why there is growing
concern among governments about the need for a certain degree of
uniformity as regards internal taxation on Central American goods is
precisely the possibility that anarchy of national action in this field
may frustrate the unimpeded functioning of free trade. As for international economic relations, it is fairly clear that some kind of accommodation must be reached with the United States government, if
any headway is to be made in the application of some of the mechanisms
devised by the Central American governments for the purpose of
ensuring balanced growth among countries in the field of manufacturing.[10]

To be sure, due process along the lines described above, and based upon the methods of inquiry, joint confrontation, and experimentation, will not guarantee the success of the Central American integration program. The consolidation of the regional economic union will continue to require bold decisions on the part of the participating governments, and it will surely develop within the rough and tumble of spirited conflict, always uncertain of the results of the current or of the next battle. Due process is not offered here as a substitute for these things which are the stuff that human problems are made of. There is reason to hope, however, that by furnishing the beginning of a system of rules of the game, due process will provide a higher degree of probability to find reasonable solutions and to ensure the continuing growth of economic integration.

Footnotes to Chapter 10

1. Multilateral Treaty, Articles VIII and XXIV; General Treaty, Articles VI, X, XI and XIX; Agreement on Integration Industries, Articles IV and VII, and Agreement on Tax Incentives, Article 3.

2. Commons, op. cit., pp. 134-42.

3. Agreement Establishing the Central American Bank for Economic Integration, Articles 2 (d) and 42; United Nations, Economic Commission for Latin America, Report of the Central American Economic Co-operation Committee (E/CN.12/672) (New York, 1964), Appendix I; and Report of the Ninth Session of the Central American Economic Co-operation Committee (E/CN.12/752) (Santiago, Chile, 1966), /mimeographed/.

4. See Report of the Central American Economic Co-operation Committee (E/CN.12/672), op. cit., pp. 16-7 and 67.

5. Commons, op. cit., pp. 83-100.

6. See Chapter 12 below.

7. For example, the interconnection and combined development of electric power systems between El Salvador and Honduras and Costa Rica and Nicaragua; joint planning and supervision of construction works of international bridges and regional highways between Guatemala and

El Salvador and Honduras and Nicaragua (see above, Chapter 8, footnote 4), and the proposal for a single farm prices stabilization institute to serve both El Salvador and Honduras (see Permanent Secretariat of the General Treaty, Annual Report 1963-64, p. 41).

8. As was done, for example, in the evaluation and reorientation of ESAPAC (1961-62) and of ICAITI (1963-64). See Report of the United Nations Mission to Study ICAITI (New York, 1963), and ESAPAC, Report of the Director to the Board (San José, Costa Rica, November, 1963).

9. See, for example, Soley Güell, op. cit., Vol. I, pp. 220-1 and 264-5; Monterrey, op. cit., pp. 518 and 520, and Alfonso Rochac, Evolución Monetaria Salvadoreña, Tres Ensayos sobre Historia Monetaria (San Salvador: Universidad de El Salvador, Instituto de Estudios Económicos, 1961), pp. 18-9.

10. The United States government has expressed dissatisfaction with the Agreement on Integration Industries, considering that it is contrary to its trade policy objectives. It has also barred the utilization of U. S. loan funds in financing integration industries, as this might result in the use of American tax money to provide special advantages to particular American interests at the expense of other American competitors.

11 DEVELOPMENT OF
CENTRAL AMERICAN
INSTITUTIONS

The Crucial Role of Regional Institutions

Strong Central American institutions are essential for the continued success of the program for economic integration. They are the
vehicles, the mechanisms that, together with the private sectors, will
have to translate legal texts into actual economic processes. It is
through their operations that the common market will be made secure
and that future growth within integration will take place.

External cooperation from various sources will continue to play an
important role in the field of research, in certain aspects of the work
needed to develop new areas of action and in the provision of financial
and technical resources. However, its role will change as the need
arises to strengthen the Central American institutions and to provide
them with adequate orientation and substantive capabilities. To be
sure, much more external cooperation will be needed than is being obtained at the present time. But from now on the critical factor for the
success of the program is the success of its own institutions.

The main implication of this proposition should be realized in all
five Central American countries: It is necessary to assign, on a permanent basis, an adequate and increasing amount of resources to these
institutions, so as to enable them to discharge their responsibilities effectively. This must be viewed not as a gift or as an extraordinary
expense of the national government, but as a profitable investment in
a joint enterprise. This is what it takes to make sure that they remain
truly and wholly Central American institutions.

On the assumption that sufficient financial resources will be forthcoming, institutional development in economic integration hinges on
three questions: (a) making the existing structures work with a

reasonable measure of efficiency (b) establishing adequate relationships among them and between them and their national counterparts and (c) providing dependable ways for the creation of new institutions. In examining these questions, a distinction should be made between agencies created by the five governments mainly to perform specialized services on their behalf--the Central American Bank (BCIE), the Institute for Industrial and Technological Research (ICAITI) and the School of Public Administration (ESAPAC)--and the central policy-making and administrative organs, charged with regulation of national actions with respect to the operations of the common market and the general issues of economic integration: The Central American Economic Council, the Executive Council and the Permanent Secretariat (SIECA).

The Need to Concentrate Institutional Action

In the case of BCIE, ICAITI and ESAPAC, the first requirement is that they concentrate rather than disperse their actions. This will enable each of these institutions to allocate rationally the resources at its disposal and to fix the necessary guidelines for the development of its organization. It will also help them to be more selective in their attempts to absorb external co-operation, thus avoiding the unbalancing effects of some offers of assistance which, even if well intentioned, may not correspond to what is needed at a given time.

Concentration of efforts will be facilitated by the fact that these institutions have been given specific tasks within well defined fields. The main function of the Central American Bank is to promote and finance industries of regional scale and public works for the common market. The assimilation and adaptation of the technological elements needed to give regional dimensions to productive activity define the field in which ICAITI must center its efforts. The development of an efficient administration in each country for the various treaties on economic integration constitutes the main target of ESAPAC's activities.

In the case of BCIE and ICAITI the need for concentration applies not only to their directly promotional programs, but also to those which they carry out in response to private demands. This means that their financing activities and their technical services should conform to an explicitly stated policy defining areas of productive endeavor, priorities and conditions for their availability, and should not be the passive reflection of such demands. As for the technical assistance, the premise here is that ICAITI must specialize in the provision of services required by economic integration, just as BCIE is supposed to deal exclusively with projects of a regional nature.

Generally speaking, therefore, these institutions should resist the pressures to broaden their actions, so long as they are engaged in developing the necessary capabilities to discharge their main and more immediate responsibilities. This is not only a function of the amount of financial resources and the competence of their technical and adminis-trative personnel. It is also a function of time, as it will depend on experience and the adequate articulation of these means.

However, the importance of developing first rate technicians and administrators cannot be underestimated. No effort should be spared in this task. A vigorous and continuous training program should be insti-tuted according to the highest standards, including the most exacting selection requirements, graduate university studies and on-the-job training both at home and abroad. Excellence is an essential prerequi-site if the regional institutions are to command the respect of national institutions and to provide the needed co-operation in the task of gearing them to the conditions established by the common market.

Relationships among National and Regional Institutions

This brings up the question of the relationships between BCIE, ICAITI, ESAPAC and the national institutions in the member countries. Here, the main concern is not integration of regional actions with efforts already being made at the national level in these fields; the tasks are new, in the sense that they did not exist previously in the five countries. Hence, it is not a question of avoiding duplication, but rather of providing useful, supplementary elements in the national effort toward institutional adjustment. The adjustment will range widely, but its immediate requisites are found in the fields of banking, balance of payments, industrial development and administrative reform.

Gearing the workings of the national banking systems and adjusting balance-of-payments policies to the requirements of free trade will be done through the co-operative arrangements being evolved by the central banks.[1] But there should be a connection in the area of investment policy between the actions of BCIE and those of the national banking systems and government bodies in charge of public works programs, for the purpose of reinforcing their mutual influence toward channeling resources to regional projects. Working interrelationships must also be established in the field of industrial development policy between BCIE and ICAITI on the one hand, and the national development institutes on the other. ESAPAC must work more closely with the governments in improving their administrative procedures and organization in fields such as customs administration, internal revenue, tax incentive laws, regional highway construction programs, and farm price stabilization schemes.

The need for a much greater degree of integration--programatic and operational--among the Central American institutions themselves, including also the Economic and Executive Councils, is being felt increasingly. This is essential for the adequate functioning of the common market and more generally for the satisfactory operation of the various regional treaties.

The Central American Bank's credit facilities are required in the process of enlarging the scope of free trade--a field under the supervision of the Economic and Executive Councils--, so as to include productive activities which are now subject to temporary restrictions and which must modernize their methods of production. The technical services of ICAITI are also needed in this process. Moreover, ICAITI is legally required to render technical assistance to both Councils in the application of uniform tax incentives and of the Agreement on Integrations Industries.[2] It will be difficult to promote regional industrialization unless BCIE and ICAITI co-ordinate their corresponding efforts. The operations of free trade and tariff equalization, as determined by the Councils, will often have a direct bearing on the credit policy of the BCIE. The Councils, in turn, must rely on ESAPAC to co-operate in improving and adjusting national administrative structures to the requirements of the common market.[3]

Building this network of interrelated actions poses delicate operational problems. The starting point must be that each institution is responsible for the discharge of its statutory responsibilities as it sees fit and as best it can. This comes before instituting any kind of co-ordination with the others. Then joint and interrelated actions, growing out of experimentation, must be developed with reference to the specific situations into which their need is rooted and in the form of concrete reciprocal demands, and not on the basis of an amorphous body--the co-ordinating committee in its various forms--in which responsibility is dissolved and accountability disappears.

The Strategy for Institutional Innovation

There seems to be a certain amount of weariness in some circles, even among governments, about creating new Central American institutions. This feeling arises as a result of the rapid developments of the last few years and of the difficulties encountered in making the existing ones work. However, it is obvious that these are only the first components of a whole constellation of institutions devoted to the economic integration of these countries. A regional organization for highway maintenance, a fisheries institute, a telecommunications authority, a geological and water resource research service are only a few of the ones being considered at present.[4]

The need for these services existed before the creation of the common market, and their lack or deficiencies at the national level is one of the most serious obstacles to the formulation and implementation of national and regional development projects. Economic integration now makes it possible to establish and operate them jointly, with greater efficiency and at lower costs for the participating countries. In other words, it offers an opportunity to realize the same kind of economies of scale in public services as it does in private productive activities.

There is no question, therefore, that new institutions will be needed. The problem, rather, is to determine which ones and when and how they are to be established.

Probably the most dependable way of effecting institutional changes is to fix the process at the growing points in the going concern of economic integration, as it establishes additional demands, with reference to the problems it encounters in its functioning. This will furnish directly useful guidelines for determining the nature of the issues in its relationship to integration, the kind of action required and the sequence and priorities to be adopted.

The existing regional institutions can play an important role in the establishment of new ones. This should include not only the basic studies but also their launching on an experimental basis and, in some cases, the initial phases of their development. This is a method used successfully in the institutional development of contemporary Mexico by agencies such as the Central Bank and the National Development Corporation (Nacional Financiera). It was the method adopted by the central banks of the region, in utilizing the facilities provided by BCIE for establishing the Central American Clearing House.[5] It recommends itself as the procedure to be followed also, as regards the need for BCIE's initiative in the creation of a capital market of Central American scope. The same is true of ICAITI's role in the establishment of the institutional base for specialized industrial research facilities in the various countries and for a wide-ranging process of investigation of the region's mineral and water resources.

There are several reasons why this line of action should be followed. In the first place, the existing institutions have absorbed most of the available trained personnel in Central America. The creation of new ones, therefore, implies creating, at the same time, the required managerial resources and top executive staffs. While this is being done, the older institutions can provide the administrative overhead for the experimental and first operational phases. In the second place, the risk of early failure or slow growth can be avoided or reduced to a minimum if the new institutional initiatives develop under the protecting framework of the stronger ongoing structures of the program. Finally, this procedure also helps to establish working relationships between the existing and the new activities, which are likely to survive, once the latter are detached into separate institutions operating on their own power.

The major proposition underlying the previous observations is that not one but several strong institutional centers should be developed for the provision of services in the process of economic integration and that their operations should be adequately integrated among themselves and with respect to national agencies. The same is true of the institutions designed to regulate national action at the regional level.

The Economic Council and Executive Council are equipped to deal with certain types of problems and not with others. The former is made up of the Ministers of Economy, while the members of the latter are in fact officials of these same ministries. They can handle issues related to the tariff, free trade, customs administration and commercial policy. But they are not empowered nor do they have the technical resources to deal with other aspects of the integration program, such as transportation, electric power, agricultural development,and certain phases of industrial policy. The institutions which can handle these matters at the Central American level are the Ministries of Public Works and Communications, the Ministries of Agriculture, the electrification institutes,and the development corporations. These will have to be brought effectively into the program

for economic integration if, for example, the common market road
network is to be completed, interconnection of national electric
power systems is to take place,and free trade is to be achieved with
respect to farm products requiring regional co-ordination of national
production and price policies.

Several meetings of officials of cabinet rank have been held,
such as those of the Ministers of Agriculture (1964) and of the
Ministers of Labor (1964).[6] The results of these meetings have shown
once more the need for previous careful research and preparatory work
by government officials at the technical level. It is because this need
was fulfilled, that success was achieved in 1963 in reaching the first
firm agreements between El Salvador and Honduras for the interconnection of their main electric power system. Similar arrangements
were made among the five governments for the completion of a regional
road network between 1964 and 1970. In both cases the decisions were
grounded on the results of research and joint discussions conducted
from time to time over the previous five years by the CCE's Sub-
Committees on Electrification and Transportation.[7]

In general, the technical subcomittee has proved to be one of
the most useful instruments in the program for economic integration.
In addition to the groups just mentioned, the Trade Subcommittee did
the preparatory work for the regional agreement on free trade and the
common tariff. In yet another field, the Statistical Co-ordination
Subcommittee has been one of the driving forces behind the development of national statistical services in the five countries under
reasonable conditions of comparability and reliability.[8]

These experiences point strongly to the advisability of setting up
technical groups to continue the work in various fields--trade,
transportation, housing, agriculture, electrification and water
resources,and statistical co-ordination--and to develop future
activities on the basis of the results they have achieved to date.
Additional bodies will have to be created to deal with new aspects of
economic integration, beginning probably with the immediate
establishment of one for fiscal policy and one for industrial development.[9]

The Need for Additional Central American Institutions

Technical subcommittees, however, are not enough in the task
of enlarging the going concern of economic integration. They can

only study the problems and prepare the way for joint action. Carrying it out may require the organization of new institutions to perform services on behalf of the governments, such as the proposed regional authority for road maintenance, or to regulate national action, such as the periodic meetings of Ministers of Public Works and Communications, to work out priorities and timetables for national programs with regional criteria.

The need for innovation is large,as the problems become increasingly complex. Free trade and tariff equalization have determined changes in the relatively simple operations of customs systems that have been in existence for a long period. They have not required any significant development in acquiring new skills and technologies, in establishing new forms of organization or in building costly additional investments. Although these systems must be modernized, this is not due to the integration treaties, but to the need to streamline the archaic organizations dealing with the legal and administrative processes of imports and exports. What the treaties as such require is uniformity among countries in their application and a permanent and dependable adjustment in the behavior of public officials with respect to the transactions of intraregional trade.

These same requirements will have to be satisfied in whatever new agreements the General American countries work out. As they move into new fields, these agreements will apply to a larger number of more difficult operations. Some of them will be entirely new, and most will necessitate the development of additional skills, the assimilation of technological experience, the establishment of new organizations and the making of relatively large investments. Various types of joint and interrelated actions will be required. For example, the formulation of regional public works programs must be done jointly, with the technical staff available at the Central American level for the basic studies. The emerging proposals will then be examined by the appropriate subcommittee and eventually by the Economic Council or by the meeting of the Ministers concerned. Here decisions will be made for the adoption of the programs in the form of recommendations to the governments, which may spell out priorities, time tables, co-ordinating bodies, as well as methods and sources of internal and external financing. The latter arrangements will, of course, have to be worked out with Ministers of Finance, and, when required, with the assistance of the Central American Bank.

So far, these actions correspond to what has been done already in other areas of economic integration. But it is precisely at this point that new developments are called for. If these activities are really to grow into truly regional programs, they will have to be jointly implemented, at least in part. This refers for example to the need to obtain external financing, for which the BCIE could well act as agent for the five governments. At the present time, this process is left largely to the initiative, ingenuity, and luck of each government, which is not a very good way of ensuring uniform and opportune compliance with priorities and timetables agreed upon jointly by all of them.

It would appear that in the immediate future the construction phases of regional public works will be generally effected at the national level. However, there will be ample opportunity here for the bilateral commissions to contribute to their success, as well as to develop experiences that might be generalized in the future throughout the integration program. Their field of discretion is now limited to the construction of bridges over international rivers, to the determination of the precise points of interconnection of regional highways, and to the supervision of the rates of progress of the respective projects according to time schedules jointly established.[10] But if successful, the bilateral commission could in time be utilized as a vehicle to pool and mobilize throughout the region the very scarce technical personnel working in the various countries. It could also be used singly or collectively to strengthen Central America's capabilities in building its own public works, such as highways, electric power systems and port facilities. This they could do either through their own organizations, or by stimulating the development of construction companies of regional dimensions.

The Co-ordination of Action toward Economic Integration

With the development of several strong centers engaged in processes of economic integration, the need arises for an overall view to be brought to bear upon their operations. This need can be already observed with respect to the articulation of the actions of the BCIE, ICAITI and the Executive Council into a coherent regional policy and will increase as the common market grows and diversifies. The General Treaty assigns this task to the Economic and Executive Councils.[11] But this they cannot discharge adequately and fully. For, as noted earlier, the members of these councils are the heads of the Ministries of Economy or their subordinates. As such, they can only provide policy direction at the regional level on matters under the jurisdiction of these ministries. They cannot do so on other matters, since it would mean invading the domain of the heads of other government departments, who are their hierarchical equals in each country, and over whom they have no statutory authority. Thus, a dual situation exists in fact, if not in the letter of the law as provided in the General Treaty.

There is no quick or easy solution to this problem, whose implications go beyond the sphere of economic affairs. The needed formulas must be sought in the broader context of all Central American organizations and institutions. This will require, among other things, reformulation of the basic conceptions prevailing at the present time about the structure and functioning of a going concern of regional affairs, for the purpose of developing a full-fledged and effective Organization of Central American States.

In the meantime, the Economic and the Executive Councils will have to cope with the situation as best they can, keeping a total picture of the program's activities, with detailed and up-to-date information on all of them, and promoting coherent and mutually reinforcing approaches by persuasive means, rather than by the authoritative application of the corresponding clauses of the General Treaty. Moreover, the members of the Economic Council are also members of the respective national political cabinets. In this capacity they are not in a position to determine unilaterally what must be done in areas outside their jurisdiction, but they can influence these decisions, and certainly ought to be able to avert major contradictions. Periodic meetings of the Economic Council with the heads of other government departments can also be a useful instrument for dealing with matters of common interest requiring joint decisions. Several meetings of this kind were held between 1963 and 1965, with the joint participation of the Ministers of Economy and the Ministers of Public Works, Finance and Agriculture, respectively.

As was mentioned earlier, the effectiveness of these meetings and indeed of any co-ordinating action at the regional level depends in large measure on the quality of the preparatory work done by the technical bodies. Here a key element of success is the strengthening of the Permanent Secretariat. Obviously, the Secretariat cannot and should not duplicate the work of the specialized regional institutions. But it should have enough experienced personnel in fields such as finance, transportation,and industrial development, so as to enable it to provide the required technical and substantive guidance.

How far the Permanent Secretariat can go in this direction is open to the same kind of questions that were raised with respect to the Economic Council as the co-ordinating body at the political level. To be sure, the Secretariat has been given a personality of its own in the General Treaty.[12] Over the past five years it has in fact developed as an instrument that the five governments use in a representative capacity in matters of economic integration. However, the moral of historical experience old and new, is also applicable here: As long as the common market remains in its initial phases, it is better to concentrate rather than to disperse action, and as long as jurisdictions are not differentiated well enough, the strength of the Secretariat is the strength which the member governments accord it and the strength which it can muster together with the Economic and Executive Councils.

Footnotes to Chapter 11

1. See Banco Central de Reserva, Acuerdo para el establecimiento de una Unión Monetaria Centroamericana (San Salvador, 1964), /mimeographed/.

2. Agreement on Tax Incentives, Article 6; Agreement on Integration Industries, Article IX.

3. ESAPAC, Director's Report to the Board, (November 1963), op. cit.

4. See above, Chapter 8, footnote 4 and Central American Research Institute for Industry, ICAITI as a United Nations Special Fund Project: Request for a Reinforced Extension of the Project for the Period July 1, 1965 to June 30, 1968 (Guatemala, November 1964), pp. 16-20.

5. Central American Bank for Economic Integration, Agreement, Article 40, and First Annual Report, 1961-62, pp. 45-6.

6. See SIECA, Informe de la Primera Reunión de Ministros de Agricultura (SIECA/RMA-I/33) (Guatemala, February 1964), and ODECA, Acta de la Primera Reunión de Ministros de Trabajo y Previsión Social de Centroamérica (San Salvador, April 1964).

7. See United Nations, Economic Commission for Latin America, Informe de la Reunión de Funcionarios de Electrificación (E/CN.12/CCE/107) (Mexico City, 1957); Informe de la Primera Reunión del Subcomité Centroamericano de Electrificación (E/CN.12/CCE/SC.5/4) (Mexico City, 1959) and Report of the Central American Economic Co-operation Committee. Sixth Session (E/CN.12/533) (Mexico City, 1959), p. 21.

8. See United Nations, Economic Commission for Latin America, Informes de la Primera a la Sexta Reuniones del Subcomité de Coordinación Estadística del Istmo Centroamericano (Mexico City, 1955, 1956, 1957, 1958, 1963 and 1964).

9. See United Nations, Economic Commission for Latin America, Report of the Ninth Session of the Central American Economic Co-operation Committee, op. cit.

10. See United Nations, Economic Commission for Latin America, Informe de la Segunda Reunión del Subcomité Centroamericano de Transportes (E/CN.12/CCE/307) (Mexico City, June 1963), p. 29.

11. General Treaty, Articles XX, XXI and XXII.

12. General Treaty, Articles XXIII and XXIV.

CHAPTER **12** TOWARD
A SECURE
COMMON MARKET

The Common Market as the Framework for
Further Economic Integration

The relative success of Central American economic integration must
be measured to a large extent against the every day operation of the
common market. This is particularly important now that the Central
American treaties are undergoing the first real tests, as the clash and
pressures of old and new interests arise. The repetitive occurrence of
expected performance will reaffirm the initial political decisions and
lay the foundations for achieving new major objectives, such as the
abolition of customs among the five countries, the generalization of free
trade to include all goods, Central American and imported, as well as
total mobility of factors of production.

The translation of the treaties into actual economic processes does
not occur automatically upon their signature and ratification. It entails
the establishment of a network of market connections for the orientation
and adjustment of supply to the structure and dimensions of regional
demand. A large contribution must be made by the private sector in
this task; but substantial public action will be called for also, much in
the same way that gaining access to the export markets in the nineteenth
century necessitated wide-ranging legal, economic and institutional
developments.

The task now is larger and more complex, in that it does not
consist only of gaining access to an existing market, but of creating the
regional market itself as a going concern, and of accommodating it in
relation to the national and international markets. The behavior of the
various parties involved in economic transactions must be adjusted in
accordance with the treaties, loading it, so to speak, in favor of
economic integration. Security of expectations on the part of the

member governments and of the private sectors with respect to this
behavior requires that the adjustment is permanent and that procedures
for further change are adequate and known. Thus the need arises to
spell out the expected behavior of the parties to the transactions of
intraregional trade, by means of the development of the main treaties
in terms of additional, more detailed, specific and operational working
rules.

The Consolidation of Free Trade

By and large, free trade and tariff equalization have worked well
so far. But security of expectations refers to future performance. Adequate performance now is not enough; it must be dependably projected
into transactions that have yet to take place. This is done by means of
rules and norms spelling out what adequate performance is and what is
to be done when it is not achieved, when conflicts or difficulties arise.
It seems to be a better procedure than improvising every time action is
called for.

Evidently, if it is to be useful, this process of additional rule
making must grow out of the actual operations of the common market
and of the methods that have been successful thus far. Its subject
matter has been anticipated to a considerable extent by the main
treaties, which call for bylaws and additional regional legislation. But
situations have risen and will rise in the future, which could not be
foreseen at the time the treaties were signed.

The basic condition that must be fulfilled with respect to free
trade is its continuity over time. The General Treaty provides, in
fact, that free movement of goods shall continue unimpeded--subject
only to the posting of bond--even when questions arise as to their
origin or the possible existence of unfair competition.[1] But this refers
only to violations of the Treaty rules. For the bulk of the transactions
of intraregional trade, made in conformity with these rules, security of
expectations with respect to the flow of trade hinges on tariff classification, verification of origin and application of quarantine and other
regulations. At the present time these operations are effected by
national authorities. In the absence of uniform procedures and common
mechanisms, unilateral action results sometimes in conflicts--on account
of divergent criteria--between the national authorities and the private
interests involved, or between member governments. These are adjudi-
cated by the Permanent Secretariat, the Executive Council or, if
necessary, by the Economic Council of the General Treaty.

The adjudication has been successful in most cases so far, in the
sense that it has provided for reasonably satisfactory settlements. But it
is costly and wasteful of time and resources. Moreover, the recurrence
of conflicts of this kind tends to instill doubts and uncertainties in the
minds of traders and investors in the regional market. The aim,
therefore, should be to avoid conflicts as much as possible and to use
adjudication only as a measure of last resort.

Substantial progress toward this end can be made by means of
(a) rulings on tariff classification, (b) uniform norms for the determination
of origin, and (c) application of uniform trade mark laws, quarantine
regulations, public health norms, and standards for industrial products.

Article XI on the Agreement of Tariff Equalization calls upon the
Central American Trade Commission--now the Executive Council--to
study and advance proposals designed to achieve and maintain the uniform application of the common tariff nomenclature. In addition,
Article V of the General Treaty provides that "The Executive Council
shall lay down regulations governing the procedure to be followed in
determining the origin of goods". These questions have been discussed
by the Executive Council on various occasions. As a result, it has been
decided: (a) to postpone the adoption of the above-mentioned regulations in order to gain additional experience on the subject; (b) to deal
with the cases that may arise on an ad hoc basis, and (c) to carry out
studies covering the rules of origin that might be applied to selected
goods corresponding to productive activities of greater and more
immediate interest to Central America's industrial development.

Rulings on classification, properly generalized with respect not only
to a regional producer but also to the product itself whatever its origin,
would make effective the tariff differential with respect to imports, in
addition to ensuring the continuity of free trade for Central American
products within the common market. Both the rulings and the norms of
origin could be made mandatory to customs authorities at all borders.
They could be issued by the Executive Council according to specified
procedures. Administratively, this might be one of the functions that
the Permanent Secretariat could perform under appropriate delegation
from the Council, in accordance with Article XXIV of the General
Treaty, except for cases of conflict which could go to the Council
on appeal.

Adoption and utilization of these instruments would require the
formulation of concrete procedures to classify goods according to the
common tariff nomenclature and to ascertain their origin. In turn,

implementation of these procedures would necessitate the establishment of a technical unit within the Secretariat and of adequate facilities at ICAITI, with appropriate supporting connections in both cases with international and other outside institutions specialized in these fields.

The Need for Uniform Trade Mark and Quarantine Legislation

Trade mark legislation, operating at the national level within the common market, makes it possible for firms manufacturing identical or similar products in a given country to register in their own name competitive trade marks from other member territories. Fortunately, the practice has not spread widely throughout Central America, but its effects upon the expansion of intraregional trade are obviously quite unfavorable whereever and whenever it occurs. This affects not only particular productive activities, but also the general degree of confidence which the business community can place upon the legal promise of a larger number of customers for their output. At the same time, it is unfair to limit in this way the market connections of firms established on the basis of efforts persistently exerted over many years, since their future depends vitally upon the unimpeded growth of such connections. On the other hand, quarantine and other sanitary norms and regulations can be used to stop or interfere with the free flow of goods among common market members, for reasons other than the control of plant and animal disease or the protection of the public health.

It seems advisable, therefore, to adopt uniform Central American trade mark legislation, quarantine regulations, and norms and standards for industrial production and to enforce them by means of regional authorities. This is a source of increasing concern in the private sector, especially among producers of drugs, cosmetics and pharmaceutical products. As for trade marks and quarantine, the Executive Council has already acknowledged the need for uniform legislation. A draft agreement on the former has been prepared and concrete proposals have been made to OIRSA on the latter, but no real progress has been made so far in these fields.

None of these questions is politically sensitive, so that their inclusion in the area of Central American action should be comparatively simple. Moreover, the gains to be derived from such an approach are large, in the task of making free trade secure from the arbitrary application of national regulations and, more generally, of establishing conditions of certainty and dependability in the operations of the common market. This could lead, in turn, to interesting institutional developments of economic integration, by increasing the effectiveness and broadening the operations of existing instruments, such as OIRSA.[2] It would also stimulate the unification and improvement of commercial laws and industrial regulations, thus creating better conditions for trade and investment in the region.

Renegotiation of Uniform Duties on Imports

Rulings on tariff classification would make for continuity and uniformity in the application of the common tariff on imports. Uniform tariff legislation[3] will perform a similar function. Important as these elements are, however, the basic issue in tariff equalization refers to the adequacy and dependability of the procedures to be used in changing uniform duties, so as to adjust them to new conditions. The present inflexible and lengthy procedures have been a matter of great concern for the governments almost from the time that the common tariff went into effect.

So far this lack of flexibility seems to be critical mainly with respect to the protection of Central America's industrial activities. It is alleged that under present arrangements it is not at all unlikely that businesses in need of immediate help will get it too late, if at all. Specifically, the difficulty seems to be centered in the naturally slow processes of legislative ratification. On this basis it is often proposed that the solution to the problem consists in doing away with legislative ratification of the tariff equalization protocols on renegotiated uniform duties.

The situation is not that simple and the solution not that easy. On the one hand, this line of thought is dangerous, as it would soon find it expedient to do away with legislative participation in the integration process and, for that matter, with anything that stands in the way of the decisions of Central American institutions. On the other hand, there are other aspects of equal if not greater importance than industrial protection that must be considered in revising the common tariff. Changes in the uniform duties will affect, in varying degrees, government revenues, the balance of payments and the welfare of consumers. This is why, in approaching the question of tariff revision, it seems advisable to start out with the principle that uniform duties are not subject to sudden changes and that when the need for adjustments arises changes will be made according to known and specific procedures.

Two considerations must be made in this connection. First, if the police power not of one but of five states is to be applied in a particular area, as is the case with the tariff, it is only reasonable to make sure that there is legitimate cause to grant such protection, by means of devices such as public hearings and research studies of various kinds and sources. Second, now that the traditional procedures and lines of access have been altered in the field of tariff policy, it is only fair that those who are directly affected be aware that there is a possibility to effect changes in uniform duties, that they have an opportunity to do something about them and know what to do and how to go about this business, in terms of operations that must be publicly known as regards their nature, timing, and sequence.

This is now an area of uncertainty in the workings of the common market. And this is why it is necessary to supplement the very rudimentary procedures which have been used in each country, as well as those that are now being utilized at the regional level, with a modern set of rules specifying the several investigational processes to be effected and the periods within which action will be taken at various levels.

These periods could refer, for example, to (a) the decision by the Executive Council, (b) the signature of protocols to the Agreement on Tariff Equalization, (c) their submittal to the national legislatures, and (d) the deposit of the instruments of ratification. As for legislative action, it should not be difficult for each national congress to adjust its internal regulations in such a way as to assign first priority to these protocols and to process them under a waiver of the normal procedures for other legislation. In addition, it would be useful for the Executive Council to have frequent contact with members of the legislative committees dealing with these matters, so that they become actually-- as they should within their own sphere of activities--part and parcel of the going concern of economic integration.[4]

A set of rules formulated along these lines should suffice to attain the required flexibility as regards the general case, within a much needed framework of stability for the common tariff. In addition, new productive activities requiring tariff protection can be aided by the recently established system of forward tariffs. This is a system whereby (a) a relatively low tariff is levied on imports of certain products--

mainly industrial raw materials, intermediate and capital goods--as long as they are not manufactured in Central America, and (b) a protective uniform duty is established in advance, to replace the former when production starts in the area with a capacity of at least 50 per cent of regional demand.[5]

This set of rules obviously would not provide the means to deal adequately with situations arising from dumping practices that are sometimes used in international trade, in this case on the part of firms exporting into Central America. Special procedures should be adopted following the rules of GATT to cope with these special situations. Although some of them have been established, the need here is to develop them in detail and to generalize their application to all productive activities that might require them, regardless of their tax and legal status within the common market.[6]

General norms of the type suggested above, however, may have to be supplemented with temporary procedures in order to deal with cases requiring rapid corrective action in the present phase. In this connection, it should be pointed out that in the original negotiations it was not infrequent that uniform duties were fixed with insufficient economic data and according to rather rough guidelines. It is, therefore, possible that the application of the new duties would endanger the chances of survival of certain productive activities, as has already happened in several cases. The ensuing need for almost immediate correction could perhaps be fulfilled by means of a temporary protocol to the Agreement on Tariff Equalization covering a period of say two or three years as a maximum. Such a protocol would empower the executive branch of the national governments to alter uniform duties, as approved by the Economic Council under its investigational processes and deadlines, within a specified maximum percentage of their current level.

In this way, the constitutional question of delegation of legislative power could be avoided, and an efficient procedure established to effect the required corrections in the tariff at the right time. After that maximum period had elapsed, the general rules would become fully applicable, as regards the participation of national legislatures or of the Central American legislative mechanisms that might have been created in the meantime.[7] There does not seem to be any need to maintain the special procedures once those corrections are made since, from the standpoint of industrial development, changes in economic conditions requiring changes in the tariff do not usually take place suddenly or overnight.[8]

Perfecting the Free Trade Zone

The successful operation and administration of free trade and of tariff equalization will facilitate in no small measure the task of perfecting the free trade zone and the common tariff. It is important to abolish the temporary restrictions to free trade that are being applied to certain items, and to remove the tariff difference in the case of those still governed by national law. However, reaching this twofold objective requires the solution of some additional problems, taking into account that a substantial part of the present productive structure operates now under temporary exceptions to free trade, and that nearly 30 per cent of the region's customs revenues come mainly from imports of goods whose duties have yet to be equalized.[9]

It is true that, with respect to free trade, the General Treaty provides for the automatic elimination of most of the restrictions. But if this is to occur and to take a permanent hold, it will have to be helped along by other public actions. The transition period was established precisely for the purpose of facilitating the adjustment of existing industries to the new dimensions of the market. This adjustment involves specialization of production by plants, larger scales of operation and, in most cases, new investments, additional integration of the industries, and renewal of equipment which is often quite obsolete. The difficulty is that the required financial capacity, technological experience, and organizational ability are scarce and do not follow automatically upon the establishment of free trade; they must be made available by means of other instruments of policy.

To the extent that this adjustment is not made, the generalization of free trade could unfavorably affect various productive activities already operating under conditions of idle capacity and duplication of investment and beginning to face the threat of foreign investments within the common market. These same situations could well give rise to unsurmountable difficulties for free trade to come and stay in effect. The difficulties encountered with respect to food staples show that making free trade effective becomes an impossible task when other requirements--in this case measures to provide for the orderly marketing of these products--are lacking.[10]

The evolution of temporary restrictions toward free trade must continue unimpeded as prescribed in the General Treaty. The implication of the foregoing observations is not that they should be interfered with, but rather that they should be supplemented by a series of measures

in addition to the gradual implementation of free trade. In fact, in
some cases free trade is legally contingent upon taking these supplementary actions within specified periods.[11]

Free trade on food staples, for example, requires at the very
minimum a coherent set of price supports and a regional network of
storage facilities. In time probably it would be advantageous to extend
these actions to co-ordinated credit and development schemes. The
regional agricultural marketing programs call for investment in
additional storage capacity, working capital for the administration of
price supports, and strengthening the existing organizational facilities.[12]
They will involve the Executive Council and the Central American Bank
at the regional level, and in each country at least the institution in
charge of agricultural price estabilization and the central bank. A
protocol dealing with some of these matters was approved late in 1965
at a joint meeting of the Ministers of Economy and the Ministers of
Agriculture.

The adjustment of existing manufactures to the conditions brought
about by free trade will require adequate protection with respect to
imports--ranging from higher custom duties, to tax incentives, to
outright subsidies-- as well as credit facilities and technical services.
The regional programs of industrial specialization will involve the
Executive Council, the BCIE and ICAITI at the regional level and
such national institutions as the development institutes, the ministries
of economy and finance and the central banks. Properly organized, and
with the co-operation of the national and regional associations of
manufacturers, the co-ordinated action of these institutions would make
the needed facilities available to the private sector. The BCIE can also
facilitate the process of adjustment by spelling out, in a detailed
statement of policy, the ways in which it will implement its function of
financial assistance to business harmed by free trade, and defining in
its bylaws the types of investments or reinvestments it is prepared to
finance.

Work on the formulation of all of these programs should be greatly
intensified and the main ones at least should be in operation before the
need for them arises in actual practice. Otherwise, it is likely that
later they would have to be set up hurriedly and in an atmosphere of
suspicion of favoritism or arbitrary action. If the adjustments begin to
be made before the stresses and strains set in, it will be easier to tend
to the problems of firms which would subsequently pose the natural doubts
of a bad risk, since by definition, their very possibilities of survival

would be substantially reduced. In this way, the pressures toward noncompliance of the treaties and retrogression in economic integration would be minimized.

Completion of the Common Tariff on Imports

Completion of the common tariff on imports from the rest of the world depends upon other actions of Central American economic policy, much in the same way that perfecting the free trade zone involves additional measures in fields other than free trade. It is useful that this be realized in order to avoid wasting time in protracted negotiations aimed exclusively at the determination of uniform duties.

Several cases may be differentiated. Some of the items for which agreement on a common duty is pending,such as gasoline and motor vehicles, are very important sources of customs revenues.[13] Depending on the size of its impact, tariff equalization may well depend in these cases on the creation of alternative forms of taxing these products internally in accordance with the fiscal needs of the governments.

In other cases, the establishment of free trade is contingent upon tariff equalization on the final product, its substitutes,or intermediate goods. The adoption of a common tariff in these cases will have a direct influence on the development of various industries which are now being established or expanded with a view to supplying the common market. The obstacles encountered here arise from such factors as concern for balanced growth among countries, possibilities of survival of particular productive activities in some of the member countries under new competitive conditions, and/or the adequacy with which regional sources of supply will replace goods traditionally imported from other countries. An example of the latter situation is found in the case of oil and oil derivatives, where it has been difficult to erect a common protective tariff, partly on account of uncertainty as to how the various refineries established in recent years will fulfill Central American demand in terms of prices, regularity and quality.

In addition to the needs already examined, the Central American common market must be made secure with respect to the operations of national policy regarding foreign exchange. In this connection the central banks, working in close co-operation with the Economic Council, could formulate detailed proposals, within the framework of Article X of the General Treaty, to cope with the various situations that might arise. It is to be hoped that full convertibility can be maintained. But if it should be threatened, as a result of a protracted decline in foreign earnings, the five countries must be prepared to protect and ensure the unimpeded working of the common market, and to utilize it in such a way as to facilitate attack on the problem of external disequilibrium.

Development of an Economic Infrastructure
for the Common Market

Frequent references have been made in earlier chapters to the need to formulate and carry out jointly public investment programs of regional scope. Some of these programs must be mentioned here, inasmuch as they are intimately related to the task of creating the physical underpinnings of the common market, namely transportation and communications services.

Previous studies have provided basic information about the magnitudes and characteristics of the physical facilities required by regional road and telecommunications networks.[14] As now conceived, they have the purpose of linking production zones with consumption centers and of interconnecting the five capital cities. Road making to open up new areas and expansion of telecommunications within each country are left for subsequent phases.

The question as to what kind of regional institutions will be established to cope with these aspects of the investment and construction processes and later of the provision of public services requiring joint action has not been answered as yet. In the case of telecommunications, the proposal has been made to establish a regional authority for this purpose, but since no detailed studies have been made about its nature, functions, jurisdiction,and relationships to national institutions and national prerogatives--only about the technical aspects of the physical facilities--progress has been slow,and the possibility of serious difficulties,once the authority comes into being,has not been eliminated. The same is true of the regional authority for road maintenance, which has been discussed off and on for several years.

Some progress has been made in the field of regulation of transportation services within the region with the agreements on temporary imports of motor vehicles throughout the common market and specifications on their weights and dimensions. These regulations must be improved and customs operations with respect to vehicles and the goods they carry must be simplified if their transit through intervening countries is to be more rapid and less costly than it is now.[15]

The adoption of measures regarding the promotion of business firms providing adequate transportation services at the regional level will also facilitate this task. The efficiency of these services could be ensured through the establishment of appropriate registers, posting of bonds and sanctions for violations of the common market treaties. On the positive side, these measures will contribute to transform the primitive and rudimentary method of the individual trucker and to differentiate gradually the commercial and transportation functions in intraregional trade. In this way, it will be possible to achieve the required scale of operations in Central American transportation, to provide for a better organization of traffic among the five countries, lower freight costs, and improved conditions regarding the regularity, opportunity and quality of these services.[16]

Footnotes to Chapter 12

1. General Treaty, Articles V, XI and XIII.

2. The organization established by the Central American countries, together with Panama and Mexico, to deal jointly with problems of animal disease. It must be noted too that, given the size and geographic configuration of the Central American Isthmus, there is very little that can be done effectively at the national level to check the spread of plant and animal disease from the rest of the region.

3. The five Central American governments have agreed to adopt a "uniform tariff legislation designed to guarantee the proper application of the Central American import tariff". See Protocol to the Central American Agreement on Equalization of Import Duties and Charges (San José, Costa Rica, July 1962), Article XX.

4. Proposals similar to these were recommended to the Economic Co-operation Committee during its Ninth Session. See, United Nations, Economic Commission for Latin America, Report of the Ninth Session of the Economic Co-operation Committee, op. cit., pp. 57-8.

5. First Protocol to the Agreement on integration industries, Title IV.

6. Agreement on tariff equalization, Protocol (San José, Costa Rica, July 1962), Chapter III, and Agreement on integration industries, Article 8. Dumping inside the common market is dealt with in the General Treaty, Chapter III.

7. The need for these regional mechanisms is being felt increasingly. If the import tariff is to remain a common tariff, it is difficult to visualize any action on the part of the national legislatures other than to approve the agreements on import duties entered into by the executive branches of the five governments. The Economic Council has already requested several studies on this subject.

8. This is not the view of the Central American Economic Co-operation Committee, which, in approving the proposal for the above-mentioned Protocol, has conceived it as an instrument of permanent application. See United Nations, Economic Commission for Latin America, Report of the Ninth Session, op. cit., p. 58.

9. The relatively few products whose import duties have not been equalized as yet produce about one third of the region's customs revenues.

10. For example, exports of corn from Honduras to El Salvador have been stopped at times, by means of informal agreements between the two governments, owing to the disruption they might cause in El Salvador's production, once they reach beyond certain volumes, and to the pressures of shipments upon available storage capacity and other price support facilities in this country.

11. General Treaty, Annex A.

12. See above, Chapter 8, footnote 4.

13. For example, duties levied on gasoline and automobiles amount to more than 20 per cent of customs revenues collected on total imports.

14. See above, Chapter 8, footnote 4.

15. At the present time loading and unloading operations are repeated at the borders within a distance of a few hundred yards, so that the two national authorities may inspect the goods. Then, if the goods are being shipped to a third member country, frequently a guard must accompany the vehicle to the next border at the expense of the carrier.

16. For an analysis of the situation of various regional investment programs, as of early 1966, see United Nations, Economic Commission for Latin America, Evaluación de la Integración Económica en Centroamérica (E/CN.12/CCE/327/Rev. 1), op. cit., pp. 111-44.

CHAPTER **13** BALANCE
AMONG
COUNTRIES

The Persistent Concern for Balance
within Integration

Equitable distribution of the benefits of the common market among
the member countries has been a central concern of the integration
program since the beginning. At its first meeting in 1952, the Central
American Co-operation Committee stressed the need to "seek wide
application for the principle of reciprocity, taking into account the
location of productive activities".[1] The search for mechanisms and
procedures to give concrete expression to this principle led the government to various actions in subsequent years.

By the end of 1958 they had committed themselves to "stimulate
and promote the establishment of new industries and the specialization
and expansion of those already established in the framework of the
program for Central American economic integration," and had agreed
that "the development of the various activities which are or may be
included in the said program must be built upon bases of reciprocity
and equity, so that all and each of the Central American countries will
progressively obtain economic benefits".[2] Later, in 1960, when the
Central American Bank was created, the promotion of economic integration and of balanced growth among countries was defined as one of
its fundamental purposes.[3] More recently, in 1962, the Agreement on
Uniform Tax Incentives for Industrial Development was formulated
"according to the needs of Central America's integration and balanced
economic development".[4]

Unlike the free trade and common tariff arrangements, these
measures have not worked out in practice as well as might have been
hoped. Dissatisfaction with their performance on the part of some

countries accounts in part for the difficulties that have been encountered
in getting legislative ratification to clear the way for the application of
various treaties and protocols signed in recent years. The persistence of
this problem and the divergence of views with respect to its solution
indicate that balance among countries is a real question, requiring overt
action, and that it is not an illusion or a situation that will take care of
itself.

Original and Present Status of the Agreement
on Integration Industries

At the beginning it was thought that balance among countries could
be ensured by rationing free trade. This idea found expression in the
two instruments signed in 1958: The Multilateral Treaty regulated the
general case, wherein free trade or preferential treatment was to be
accorded without regard for the location and other characteristics of
productive activities; the Agreement on Integration Industries, on the
other hand, covered the special case and was to be used to grant free
trade in the case of major industrial activities, by means of protocols
specifying the location and various other conditions under which the
corresponding plants were to be established.

The industries that are eligible under the Agreement are defined as
those composed of one or more plants that require access to the whole
Central American market in order to operate economically even at
minimum capacity. The products of plants designated as integration
industries in the special protocols are granted the exclusive privilege
of free trade for a period of ten years; while those of plants not so
designated are subject to the payment of customs duties beginning at
the level of the common external tariff and diminishing at the rate of
10 per cent per year. In addition, the special protocols stipulate the
minimum capacity and the location of the plants by countries, as well
as quality standards, minimum-supply guarantees, tax concessions and
other conditions for their establishment and operation.

Thus, the question of the possible unfavorable effects of free trade
on balance among countries was to be solved by limiting the free trade
privilege in the case of major industries, so as to apportion them
equitably among the member countries. This function of the Agreement--
though not the Agreement itself--was superseded late in 1960. In the
General Treaty free movement of goods was generalized and regulated
independently of the issue of balance among countries, and the

Agreement on the Integration Industries was no longer a means to achieve free trade nor an instrument to generate balance by rationing free trade. The unimpeded flow of Central American goods throughout the five countries came to be the rule, subject only to the exceptions and temporary restrictions specified in the lists attached to the General Treaty.

It is important to bear this in mind, so as to get on with the task of developing a strong regional economy. To throw blocks in the path of the common market will not contribute to overcome whatever lack of balance may exist initially. Slowing down on free trade and tariff equalization is no longer possible; making them work well is important not for the mere formal purpose of complying with the 1960 agreements, but because all five countries stand to gain from it, with so many interests and activities becoming gradually involved in their operations.

It should be equally plain that balance among countries was not discarded as one of the basic principles of the program of economic integration upon the signature of the General Treaty. As already indicated, the principle was explicitly incorporated in its clauses on the industries regime, uniform tax incentives and the BCIE. It is the way to achieve balance that is now different, in that it must not endanger the secure functioning of the common market.

Overcoming Existing Imbalances through
Economic Integration

Simply stated, the problem of balance grows out of the fear that unless something is done to promote it, productive activity induced by the common market will tend to concentrate in certain member countries and that some of them will not get their fair share of the gains from economic integration. This concern has its roots in particular situations in the countries of the region, which make each of them feel that it is weaker with respect to the others.

There is, for example, the case of El Salvador, saddled with a demographic problem, the dimensions of which are unknown in the rest of Central America. There is also the case of Honduras which, unlike Guatemala, El Salvador and Costa Rica, never established an export sector of its own, and that of Nicaragua, whose export economy got on to a late start. These facts help explain why it is that Honduras has yet to build the basic elements of a road network and port facilities and why Nicaragua has not yet succeeded in attracting much direct investment from abroad; they also explain why these two countries lag behind the others as regards their entrepreneurial elements. There are other situations that are mentioned less frequently, such as the burden that Guatemala must carry on account of its segregated indian-white-mestizo structures, and the growing inability of the Costa Rican system to cope effectively with the problems that beset it internally.

These relative weaknesses are not pronounced enough to affect the denominator of underdevelopment which is common to the five countries, nor have they enabled any of them to impose lasting relationships of political or economic dependence upon the others; but they are considered to be sufficiently large as to give rise to differences in the capacity of the individual countries to take advantage of the opportunities inherent in economic integration.

Looked at from a more inclusive angle, these situations turn out to be not the obstacles but the very reasons why economic integration is being instituted in Central America. They did not arise as a result of free trade and the common tariff; they existed before as manifestations of the problems of development at the national level. This is why the unification of the Central American economies cannot be based only on free trade and tariff protection, everything else being left to its fate afterward. Other positive joint actions must be taken, if the structural weaknesses of each country are to be overcome.

Substantively, therefore, balance among countries is just another name for growth among the members of the common market and instrumentally, a policy of balance is that in which the five countries organize and co-operate among themselves to overcome the chief difficulties standing in the way of the development of each, be it population pressure in El Salvador, insufficient transport facilities in Honduras or inadequate industrial investment in Nicaragua. This is what each country needs, in addition to its own hard work, and no more. If they do not organize themselves to do it, then there is no integration and no development; if some grow, and some do not, then there is no balance among countries. But once the basic co-operative measures are taken, no limits should be placed upon the lawful efforts of all partners to take advantage of the opportunities of economic integration. This is not an enterprise in which each and every member is bound to grow at the same rate; nor can it be expected that they all maintain equal levels of development.

The concept of balance among countries, therefore, means that
all of them enjoy equality of opportunities in a process of growth made
possible by the enlarged regional market. The emphasis here is upon
opportunities, so as to shift attention to the active policies that it
takes to get results, rather than concentrating directly upon the results
themselves. This in a way would be akin to putting the cart before
the horse.

In this case, it is through joint action that equality of opportunity
will be created. And not all of it will be done on the basis of
Samaritan benevolence. It will be done because it is in the interest
of each country that the others overcome their weaknesses. Now that
the regional market begins to play an increasingly important role in
their economic development, the strength of one depends upon the
strength of the others. Letting the weak stay weak cannot be allowed,
because the market will be to that extent diminished. There is a
common interest in having everyone grow.

From Balance among Countries to
Balance among Sectors

Sharing opportunities will lead to sharing results if the five members
apply themselves well and persistently to the task of development within
the common market. This can only be done in a dynamic process which
is not to be conceived in terms of identical productive structures in each
and all five countries, or a static distribution of resources among them.
It entails rather the change of the present competitive national
economies into a set of interdependent systems bound by strong complementary relationships and by several common underpinnings in the fields
of law, public investment, and economic services. It also entails the
enlargement of their productive capacity under conditions conducive to
the free movement of factors of production within the common market.

Obviously, complementarity among the Central American economies
does not imply that some countries remain agricultural, some industrialize, and all develop into a system governed internally by colonial-
like processes. The oversimplified nature of this idea is readily
apparent to those who can visualize the magnitudes involved and who
are aware of the fact that the colonial system, as known historically,
must be based upon much wider economic, technological and military
disparities than exist in the region. What complementarity does imply,
and more important, what the very nature of the problem of growth in

Central America determines, is that it is not possible to have five major manufacturing centers, one in each country. It would be childish to think that this is possible. Even the larger Latin American countries, like Brazil, Mexico and Argentina, each of whom is several times larger than all of Central America, have so far developed only one or two of such major centers.

To be sure, the location of economic activity constitutes one of the poles of the problem of balance among countries. But it must be approached within a more inclusive framework. As regards the manufacturing sector, it is necessary to differentiate between the cores, which must be very few in number, and the subsidiary activities utilizing their products or producing their inputs, which in many cases can be decentralized. In addition, the analysis has to be broadened, so as to examine the locational problem as it relates to agriculture and its modernization, as well as to the development of transportation, financial, commercial and educational services.

It would not be surprising if, as the analysis proceeds, it was found that being near a manufacturing center and having other products and services to trade for its output may be as advantageous or even more advantageous than having such a center. The question would depend on the terms governing this trade and the substance of the problem would then shift from one of balance among countries to one of balance among sectors. This is precisely what will tend to occur as the national economies take on more and more of a regional dimension. In time, Central America could leave behind the political hurdle of alignments along purely national lines and get into a position where it could tackle the problems of its backward areas with a greater degree of flexibility.

The Need for a Common Factors Market

From the standpoint of growth, taking advantage of the opportunities of economic integration can only be done through the organization of the scarce technical, financial, and entrepreneurial resources into regional private and public enterprises, so that the Central American countries may develop supply capabilities corresponding to the dimensions of regional demand. Conditions must be created, therefore, not only to make it possible, but also to provide decisive inducements to mobilize resources in this way.

This calls for no less than the creation of a co-ordinate common factors market parallel to the common products market that is already in operation. The BCIE and ICAITI can perform a catalytic role in this task by providing research and financial services. The granting of national status by each member country to investments and construction firms from other Central American countries will also make a useful contribution.[5]

However, much remains to be done. The establishment of a truly common factors market requires more sweeping legal and economic changes in such areas as taxation, credit, migration, business,and corporation law. Little or no work has been done so far on these problems in Central America. A promising start could perhaps be made by focussing research on the concept of the regional firm or corporation, segregating it legally from other types of businesses by means of uniform working rules of Central American scope, and granting it the required differentiated treatment--both in terms of substance and procedure --through corresponding adjustments in the general norms dealing with incorporation, tax liability, credit operations, profit remittances and the like.

The implications of a common factors market from the point of view of balance among countries are obvious. Gradual progress toward full mobility of factors of production and effective movement of capital, labor, technical skills,and entrepreneurship to wherever economic opportunity may be found throughout the five countries, will contribute to overcome the imbalances that subsist as the locational patterns of productive activity develop. The need to seek balance through this additional process is readily apparent. No matter how much productive activity is established in the densely populated areas, such as El Salvador, it seems unlikely that they can achieve rapid and sustained development unless a more adequate relationship is established between people and resources on a regional basis; this requires, of course, that conditions be favorable to population movements among countries. Similarly, no matter how much investment is made in roads, port facilities and electric power in the relatively less developed areas, such as Honduras, technical and entrepreneurial resources from the outside will be needed to exploit the economic oppor-tunities thus created, through the modernization of agriculture and the promotion of industrial growth.

The organization of resources into regional enterprises will con-tribute to the emergence of a Central American interest and point of view. This will make the solution of the problem of balance to some extent independent of the question of location of productive activity, in much the same way that an inclusive approach to the question of location will tend to transform the problem into one of balance among sectors; both processes will then converge to facilitate the establishment of the needed patterns of economic activity.

As it moves away from locational considerations, the problem of balance among countries will be redefined gradually in such a way that its solution should come to hinge on (a) making the common factors market secure and (b) the articulation of national investments into larger ventures of regional scope. It would seem, at least on the surface, that making the common factors market secure could be done largely by means of the same type of measures required to attain the same objective as regards the operations of the common products market.[6]

One issue would still remain unsolved, namely the distribution of economic power among the groups that would have to combine to form the regional enterprises. In time these groups would tend to acquire a regional identity, but at the beginning they would naturally align themselves along national lines. Therefore, when national interests meet at the points of growth of regional productive activity, some terms for their reciprocal accommodation within the larger concern of economic integration will have to be worked out. Common factors and products markets provide the framework, but within these limits the entrepreneurs must define the kind of role they want to play in regional affairs and come together on specific ventures for the purpose of creating initial working arrangements. Thus another dimension of the problem of balance comes into focus: As productive activity begins to develop within regional organizations, the question of the location of its physical facilities begins to recede and to give way to a concern with the location of the corresponding economic power.

The Dynamic Nature of Balanced Growth

It follows from the preceding considerations that balance among countries is closely linked to the process of regional development. There can be no balance without development, just as there can be no distribution without production. Like development, therefore, balance is a dynamic process in that its emphasis will have to change over time from one country to another, from one area to another, as resources develop and production factors shift their geographic location. In fact, its very terms will tend to move, as already suggested, from country lines to sectoral lines and from the location of physical facilities as between countries to the distribution of economic power as between groups.

The kind of balance that is achieved will depend on the kind of development that takes place. Underlying the previous analyses, there is one conception of the program for economic integration as a Central American enterprise, built by Central Americans as a means to develop Central America's resources. There is, of course, the possibility that the common market will be utilized by foreign firms as means for maintaining their exports to these countries, through the establishment of skeleton or "ghost" industries that import the same goods with various degrees of processing and transformation. This is the pattern that is built primarily upon the alliance of national and foreign interests in one country, to defeat the alliance of national and foreign interests in another country, which is already taking place at the present time.

The centrifugal effects of activities of this kind would soon threaten the very possibilities of survival of a Central American process of economic integration. They are the same type of effects as those which contributed on the economic side to the breakdown of the federal republic, through the establishment of the export economy along state rather than federal lines. If a correct approach is used this time, genuine regional interests--both public and private--will be created. These will then begin to reach a position where they can associate themselves with foreign interests under conditions of diminishing inequality and assimilate the external resources without which development could not proceed much farther at a rapid pace.

Allocation of Industries among Countries

Balanced growth is a long-run objective, and its achievement presupposes the continued willing participation of the five countries in the program for economic integration. The way to elicit such partici- pation is to implement the instruments of balance that have been agreed upon, to put them to work with a genuine effort, making sure at all times that uniform conditions prevail where there is equality and that differential treatment is applied where there is inequality. This is not an easy task and it will not be encouraged by relatively rapid and visible results, as in the case of free trade. Nor can it be fully accomplished without a series of measures designed to ensure the free movement of factors within the regional market. Nevertheless, the General Treaty was signed in such a spirit, and compliance with its provisions on balanced growth is required in order to reach the point where the long-term measures begin to operate in actual practice.

The instruments in question fit well into the processes of balance and development. Moreover, there is general acceptance of the need for uniform tax incentives to industrial development and for a selective policy on the part of the Central American Bank, designed to equilibrate the distribution of investments within the region. This is not true of the Agreement on Integration Industries, although recent developments suggest that a working consensus on the application of this instrument may be forthcoming. Early in 1966 the Central American Economic Co-operation Committee approved a comprehensive set of procedures, whose joint implementation by the five governments would result in a vigorous and greatly intensified utilization of the Agreement.[7]

This is a promising sign, not so much because of the efficiency of the Agreement, which has yet to be tested, but because the equitable allocation of industries among countries is a real problem in Central America, as in other developing areas in which economic integration efforts are being made. For example, the recent difficulties of the East African Common Market are due mainly to the fact that Tanzania and Uganda are none too happy about the concentration of manufacturing activities in Kenya.[8] Similar concern can be observed within LAFTA, with reference to the need for agreements on industrial complementation and the problems of the less developed countries,[9] as well as in the Customs and Economic Union of Central Africa, whose Treaty states in its preamble that "the adoption of procedures for the equitable distribution of industrialization projects ... will contribute in large measure to the improvement of the standard of living of the peoples".[10]

Getting back to Central America, time may show that the Agreement on Integration Industries is an effective means for expanding free trade. It can help, for example, in the establishment of relatively large and complex industries with Central American participation, such as steel and pulp and paper, thus contributing to the emergence of actual commodity flows among countries. Time may also confirm the need to apply the Agreement in conjunction with other policy measures, so as to prevent or correct duplication of investment and waste of capital resources, as in the case of oil refining, fertilizers and other chemical industries, as well as to protect Central American producers from the irresistible pressure of foreign enterprises many times larger and more powerful.

Be that as it may, there is a need here to overcome the doctrinaire and dogmatic approach that has sometimes characterized the discussions on this subject. Too much time has been spent arguing about the pros and cons of the monopoly power that--it is said--would emerge from the application of the Agreement on Integration Industries. There seems to have been little awareness in these discussions of the fact that the determining factors of such power are to be found in the combined action of a small market and the technical and economic conditions of modern industry and that monopolistic and oligopolistic structures are characteristic of all contemporary industrialized societies. What is required instead is to experiment with concrete formulas, so as to develop the empirical bases without which it would not be possible to improve policy judgements about matters of this kind, including the efficacy of existing instruments.

Footnotes to Chapter 13

1. United Nations, Economic Commission for Latin America, Informe de la Primera Reunión del Comité de Cooperación Económica de los Ministros de Economía del Istmo Centroamericano (E/CN.12/AC.17/24) (Honduras, 1952), p. 27.

2. Agreement on Integration Industries, Article I.

3. Agreement Establishing the Central American Bank for Economic Integration, Article 2 and General Treaty, Article XVIII.

4. Agreement on Uniform Tax Incentives, Article 1 and 21 to 28, and Transitory Articles First through Fifth.

5. Multilateral Treaty, Article XVII, General Treaty, Article XVI.

6. See above, Chapter 12.

7. See United Nations, Economic Commission for Latin America, Report of the Ninth Session of the Central American Economic Co-operation Committee, op. cit., pp. 62-6.

8. East Africa, Report of the Economic and Fiscal Commission, op. cit., pp. 19-23.

9. United Nations, Economic Commission for Latin America Annual Report, 1964-65, (E/CN.12/731/Rev. 2).

10. André G. Anguilé and Jacques E. David, L'Afrique sans frontieres (Monaco (Pté): Société des Editions Paul Bory, 1965), p. 88; see also pp. 87, 89-94 and 129-50.

CHAPTER **14** THE PATTERN OF
DEVELOPMENT IN
THE NEXT STAGE

The Transformation of the Present
Productive Structure

The next stage of development in Central America will entail the transformation of the present structures of trade and economic activity through the introduction of new lines of production and the opening of new market outlets. In this sense the process will be similar in kind to the economic reorganization that took place in these countries around the middle of the nineteenth century, which has been described in Chapter 2. However, the new economy will be based to a much greater extent on internal markets and, therefore, will be different from the export economies that characterized the first stage of development of the region.

The detailed characteristics of the new economy cannot be anticipated, although the tools now available to describe the working of economic systems and the techniques of economic projection can make significant contributions toward this end. Projection requires that the nature of the relationships newly created among the five national economies be formulated explicitly and that the objectives sought through economic integration be set forth in clear terms. A broad vision of this kind also provides useful guidance as to the type of economy that is being encouraged to grow and the policies that will be required for the development of the common market.

As noted in earlier chapters, the common market was established in response to the increasing inability of five national systems to provide for the economic needs of the member countries. It is a means devised to help them develop their own potentialities.

It has been known for a long time that, relatively speaking, the region is not poorly endowed with natural resources. The descriptive literature of the nineteenth and earlier centuries is rich in comments on the plentiful supply of good agricultural lands, the diversity of climates and all of the good things that could be obtained from them through the application of hard work and careful husbandry.

Writing in 1855, two German scientists traveling in the area had this to say about Costa Rica: "The soil of Costa Rica is much more fertile than the most fertile regions in the States of Illinois, Ohio or Pennsylvania. Crops grow without fertilizer, almost anywhere, twice a year. In addition to most varieties of northern and temperate zone grains, the most useful and remunerative plants of the tropics grow here in wonderful abundance: Especially bananas, coffee, cane sugar, and cotton, yielding larger volumes and richer harvests than even in the most fertile islands in the West Indies".[1] As for the situation prevailing in the eighteenth century in the region as a whole, Virgilio Rodríguez Beteta comments as follows: "Central America experienced a languid and miserable life, in complete contrast with its wonderful geographic position and its natural resources capable of any miracle".[2]

It is now known that the areas devoted to the cultivation of coffee and cotton are among the best in the world for these purposes; that the region could develop a thriving livestock industry for its own needs as well as for export, and that its forest resources could support a wide array of industries ranging from wood production to cellulose, paper and the like.[3] Central America can produce all the food and fiber it needs and much more to sell in the international markets, including cane sugar, rice, fresh fruits, vegetables, and tobacco. The information gathered in recent years suggests the existence of a large water resource potential for multiple uses and the presence of important mineral deposits, including bauxite, iron, and copper. The opportunities that several thousand miles of sea coast offer for the development of fisheries have only begun to be grasped and the exploitation of tourist resources is still in an embryonic stage.

With all these potentialities the Central American people have not been able as yet to fulfill adequately their basic needs for food, clothing and housing. The levels of consumption are low and little diversified: In the case of food there is growing evidence that the levels of per capita consumption have suffered a deterioration in significant items over the last two decades.[4]

Among the numerous factors usually advanced as indicators of underdevelopment, the small size of internal demand and the relatively small supply capabilities seem to have played a central role in the apparent contradiction between resource possibilities and actual accomplishments. To be sure, the way in which the structure of property and government developed during the second half of the nineteenth century, in response to the newly acquired access to the main centers of the world economy, had a substantial impact on the continuing weakness of the internal market.[5] But with an export sector growing along national and not regional lines, it is difficult to visualize how the economies could have overcome the basic limitations of size. Surmounting the difficulties that these limitations throw in the path of a viable economy is the crux of the problem to which the various countries have addressed themselves with the creation of the common market.

The Diversification of Production

For reasons set forth in some detail in the first part of this study, the growth of the Central American economies can no longer be based on one or two export crops, as it was up to the great depression of the 1930's. The export sector, even under optimistic assumptions concerning future world demand for agricultural products, will not be able to provide sufficient employment opportunities to absorb population increments in these countries; nor will it be able to support a complex of growing and diversified needs. In addition, historical experience shows that economies relying excessively on a few export commodities tend to develop as simple appendices of other, foreign economies; under such conditions it is difficult to achieve and maintain a reasonable degree of political and economic independence.

The existing productive structure provides the point of departure in the effort to transform the present pattern, in which general and sectoral development depends upon the growth of one activity, into one in which growth results from the mutual reinforcement of the various components of the economy. For a long time to come, traditional exports will play a decisive role in the evolution of the Central American economies. They provide for over 500 million dollars worth of imports annually and may be expected to remain a large portion of the monetized activity. Thus any country that neglects traditional exports does so at its own peril.

There is not much that the common market can contribute specifically to increase the volume of traditional exports at the present time,
except to facilitate the development of a joint trade policy. But
economic integration stands to gain a great deal from a healthy export
sector which will provide the means for investment capital and other
essential goods needed for regional development.

The situation is different in the case of the national manufacturing
sectors and of domestic agriculture. Here regional programs of specialization and modernization can give the already established industries
dimensions commensurate with regional demand. Thus, such elements
of Central American entrepreneurship as now exist will be in a position
to survive and gain in relative strength.

Domestic agriculture will have a decisive role in expanding the
internal market by means of a rapidly increasing output of cheaper food
and raw materials. The new opportunities offered by the regional
market will make possible specialization in the location of food
staples, the diversification of production, integration and agriculture
and the livestock industry, and the increase of productivity through the
widespread utilization of modern inputs.

The development of new activities poses the question not only of
their structure as such, but also of their relationships to the present
pattern of economy and to additional diversification. If the common
market functions securely and appropriate measures are taken to promote
enterprises of regional size, these new activities can be oriented to the
needs of Central America as a whole. The present pattern of imports
and the known availabilities of the resources of the region define the
reference points in this task. The relative merits of opportunities based
on import substitution and of those which give rise mainly to exports
would thus be taken into account. In addition, a close look at the
relationship between import substitution and resource development would
make for a healthier process of regional growth.

The general aim of policy within integration is the promotion of
economic activities; but its operative concern is the establishment of
industries that serve as nuclei of economic growth. These are basic to
the achievement of a balanced, sustained and interdependent process of
regional development. As suggested earlier, production in Central
America of modern inputs for agriculture and the construction industry,
for example, would tend to free the operations of both sectors from the
limitations that may be imposed by occasional or chronic shortages of

foreign exchange. In turn, establishment of manufacturing industries for the processing of raw materials and the production of intermediate and capital goods would result in a higher degree of articulation of industries already established in this sector and would provide the core for the development of various other activities into future industrial complexes.[6]

The Required Instruments of Policy

The promotion of an integral process of growth shifts the focus of economic policy from particular commodities to the mechanisms and procedures needed to create the organization required, to enlist willing participation of the private economy and to acquire the corresponding technologies, skills and physical and financial resources. The general case can be taken care of by free trade, the common tariff, and similar instruments having pervasive effects on factor markets. Less general cases will call for additional measures providing more specific incentives and disincentives, such as special tariff protection, support prices, subsidies and tax exemptions, as well as availability of credit and technical co-operation and differential conditions for their provision. A third situation is likely to arise, in which these measures will have to be supplemented by direct governmental action. These consist of the specific promotion of particular industries through the Central American Bank, ICAITI and the national development corporations.

Mentioning general instruments, special incentives and direct governmental action in that order does not imply here a scale of preference for the adoption of policy measures to promote economic development within the common market. Each type of measure is relevant to a particular situation and can be combined with others in different ways to cope with problems calling for different degrees of public action. By the same token, increasing the efficiency of export production, modernizing domestic agriculture, specializing national manufactures and promoting the establishment of additional centers of growth, do not correspond in that order to a time sequence for the programs that are to contribute to their achievement; nor do they reflect a scale of priorities for the allocation of available resources.

This array of policy objectives reflects the view that Central American economic growth must be conceived as a many-pronged process proceeding along various lines. The weight to be assigned to each of the objectives will vary over time according to the need to promote the development of the various types of productive activity, so that they mutually reinforce the continuous growth of the economy as a whole. In this way, particular orientations of economic policy will be geared to the limiting factors operating in the economy according to their relative strengths   and will not necessarily correspond to prede-termined targets of growth for its various sectors, however logical or desirable they may be from other points of view.

Thus, for example, if a government were bent on achieving a high rate of growth of industrial output, it would do well to adopt policies designed to strengthen the internal market precisely at the points relevant for the present manufacturing structure. Similarly, policies that contribute to maintaining a dynamic export sector can facilitate the modernization of agriculture and the growth of industrial output, by providing investment funds and imports for public works and capital formation in manufacturing.

The various avenues of growth that have been mentioned define the scope of a profound process of industrialization of the Central American economy. This is what is meant by the application of scientific knowledge to the processes of production in general, the spread of technological knowledge, the growth of organic connections among sectors within the common market, the utilization of modern capital inputs and the development of skills which are in fact characteristic of an industrial society.

In creating the new industrial society, manufacturing will play a key role as the focus of relationships with other sectors of the economy. The expansion of manufacturing activities will go hand in hand with the expansion and modernization of the primary sectors, by creating new internal demands for their products and by contributing to a higher degree of processing of both traditional exports, as well as new products based on the region's forestry, fishing and mineral resources. In a very real sense, even the modernization of traditional agriculture is a process of industrial transformation in terms of the integration of agriculture and livestock production and the development of the marketing system, as well as the acquisition of more advanced skills and the increasing utilization of industrial inputs on the farm.

Continuing Importance of the Export Sector

Increased production for the home market will not diminish the importance of the export sector, which will always perform a crucial function in the development of the Central American countries. This is an inescapable fact, a historical constant that did not have to be faced by countries like Argentina and Brazil when they began to industrialize thirty years ago, because of their much larger size and the higher levels of growth they had achieved. But even these countries appear to have reached the stage where import substitution no longer provides sufficient stimuli for sustained growth.

Be that as it may, the policies of autarchy that were adopted by the larger countries, as a result of the breakdown of multilateralism, could never succeed in Central America. Unpublished preliminary estimates by the United Nations Economic Commission for Latin America suggest that the size of the common market is not at present, and is unlikely to be in the foreseeable future, large enough to warrant, as a closed economy, even the modest rates of growth adopted as the minimum targets in the Charter of Punta del Este.

The active participation of the Central American countries in the international economy is also required for other reasons. In their next stage of development they will need wide access to a vast pool of modern technology in many fields of productive activity; they will have to acquire scientific knowledge in order to adapt modern techniques to the Central American environment and will have to provide the labor force with the skills to utilize productively and profitably the new knowledge and techniques.

This task did not have to be done when developing the export economy. It would be a large task in any case. But it is now larger and more complex as a result of the fact that for over one century Central America was impervious to the great strides made by science and technology in the more advanced countries.

The Need for a Regional Trade Policy

Thus the common market does not lead to isolation. On the contrary, it will help to give the Central American economy the required productive dimensions to be successful in its foreign trade activities. The development of new export lines must have a secure base in the domestic market and productive capacity must reach a minimum level in order to gain access to overseas markets. The common market in Central America can contribute to the fulfillment of these new conditions.

However, what these countries can achieve in this direction through economic integration will face serious obstacles   unless a reasonable measure of order is established in the world economy and a minimum of opportunity opens up for the growth and diversification of their international trade. They cannot but observe with apprehension the continuing breakdown of multilateralism and the isolationist and aggressive policies being pursued by the more advanced economic centers. Should this trend continue, Central America would encounter added difficulties in utilizing the common market to promote its economic interests abroad and would be forced to orient the development of its productive structure under a more protectionist policy. This, of course, would have unfavorable effects, from the standpoint of cost and efficiency, on its development process.

The continuing importance of the external sector and the increasing complexity of its operations make it imperative for Central America to develop a modern trade policy of its own. The field is entirely open now to do this, since in creating the common market the five countries did away with previous commitments to third countries that would have interfered with the operations of intraregional trade and the common tariff. For the same reasons, the new policy must be regional in scope. [7] Thus, the need arises to evolve appropriate legal mechanisms to conduct negotiations and administer trade programs at the regional level, as well as to train and develop a professionally competent group of Central American public officials to discharge these functions. [8]

The substantive issues involved in the formulation of a regional trade policy have not yet been studied. Yet, at least on the surface it would seem that, as regards traditional exports, the Central American countries must participate wholeheartedly in the respective international commodity agreements and, within this framework, attempt to diversify their sales among the United States, Canada and the Western European countries. They would also do well to explore and take advantage of openings that may materialize for export to at least some of the socialist countries.

With respect to new exports, the problem of market access will vary. Abstracting from the questions of cost and size of productive activity, the general instruments of trade policy falling under the heading of preferential systems would probably have to be confined to Central American relations with countries of similar size and level of development. Concrete agreements, ranging from partnerships to sales

contracts with world producers, shippers,and distributors   could channel
a large portion of exports to industrialized countries, owing to their
oligopolistic practices and to the requirements of their mass production
organizations. Tariff preferences and minimum mandatory quotas could
be more widely used to regulate relationships with the more advanced
Latin American countries and other developing areas.

Two general considerations emerge in this context: The need to
make use of a wide array of tools and mechanisms in the formulation
and administration of a regional trade policy, and the increasing
complexity in the structure of markets as to their working and their
numbers. In the nineteenth century London was the market that
mattered. Then it was New York or Hamburg. Access to these markets
was comparatively easy for the one or two products involved. Now
there will be more markets, a larger number of products, with varying
and increasingly detailed specifications,and a larger number of competitors. Finally, there are also the questions, more delicate because
of their political implications, of economic association with Panama,
closer links with Mexico and the Caribbean countries,and Central
America's participation in the wider Latin American common market by
means of appropriate connections with LAFTA.[9]

The Role of Foreign Investment

An important aspect of the relationships between developing
countries and the international economy has to do with the role to be
played by private foreign investment in their future economic development. To be sure, the need for large amounts of external savings is
generally recognized. But substantial changes have occurred in the
present century among the groups and institutions involved in the
process, both inside and outside these countries.

Now the function of external savings for financing development
is viewed as supplementary to the internal investment effort. In
general, public works and the economic infrastructure no longer
absorb private capital funds from abroad; these funds are being
provided largely by international credit agencies or by individual
governments. Moreover, the development of agriculture has come to
be considered as an exclusively national endeavor, aided only by
foreign loans and external technical assistance. In this way the
emphasis upon direct foreign investment has been shifted gradually to
the areas of manufacturing and related developments of natural
resources.

Within this new orientation the prevailing attitudes also run along lines different from those of the nineteenth century. There is now a marked interest in promoting foreign investment in such a way as to achieve a reasonable participation of local capital and to ensure the development of native entrepreneurial resources and technical personnel. There is also a definite interest in seeing to it that the respective productive ventures are not only profitable in themselves, but also contribute to the general growth of the economy, in terms of economic scales of production, adequate industrial processes, the strengthened articulation of the productive structure, the avoidance of duplications and waste of capital resources,and the improvement of the balance-of-payments position.

Central American views on this subject are no exception to the general trend. They have been expressed recently (1965) in a joint statement of the Ministers of Economy, which defined in concrete terms the broad objective of policy regarding foreign investment, as the five countries begin to industrialize within the common market. It is also generally agreed that this must be a uniform policy throughout the region, recognizing the insufficiency of unilateral action and its inefficiency from the standpoint of economic integration.

The difficulties arise when it comes to deciding on the instruments that should be adopted. There are differences of opinion as to how specific and mandatory these instruments should be. However, an appreciable degree of agreement exists to the effect that the Central American Bank and the Agreement on Integration Industries could usefully serve some of the stated purposes, as they bring a public point of view to bear upon the nature and characteristics of these investments that come within their purview. On the other hand, the prevailing view, at least for the time being, is that no specific regional legislation should be enacted with a view to regulating foreign investments.

Thus it would be fair to assert that there is in Central America a definite awareness of the need for a regional foreign investment policy as well as an increasing understanding of its objectives, but that its implementation up to now has been left largely to the workings of the persuasive means that the five countries may be able to use for these purposes. It is an open question at this juncture whether such an approach will suffice in the end. Should time and experience provide a negative answer, it might be necessary for the governments to adopt more direct mechanisms of the types that have been instituted by other developing countries in the form, for example, of import permits and licencing of industrial investments.

However, much can still be done within the present constraints. There is ample room for the Central American public and private sectors to co-ordinate their efforts in an attempt to establish useful working relationships with private foreign groups and firms interested in investing in the common market. On the other hand, changes may be taking place in the outlook and orientation of some foreign investors, which cast a ray of hope on the prospects for Central America in this field.

The following remarks made recently in a private business publication are quoted here by way of illustration:

> Although to date the governments have taken a mild stand, stating that foreign capital should unite with local investors where possible, it is probable that in the not-too-distant future they will review investment proposals more selectively. The problem of proliferation of companies within the same industry is growing in importance, not only in the minds of individual Central Americans, but also in the councels (sic.) of governments and international agencies. To an extent, this is a reaction against competition, but the charge that duplication of production facilities wastes money and talent in such a small market carries weight... Possible solutions to this problem are being debated now. There is little support for statutory limitation, although this cannot be ruled out. The probable course of action is for development agencies and private development banks, as well as chambers of commerce, to act in concert to discourage overinvestment in a given field. A harsher stand, however, could follow a series of business failures. [10]

There is not much that a vigilant defender of the public welfare could reasonably find wrong in this statement.

Finally, it should be stressed that the situation in Central America at the present time is not characterized by an excess, but a shortage of foreign investment in the regional process of industrialization. This suggests the need for these countries' policies to be carried out actively and not passively, with a view to increasing the total availability of capital funds in accordance with the required conditions. An approach such as this would make it easier, by orienting the effort in specific directions as to the productive activities being promoted, to implement a course of action which, as has been seen, must proceed in selective rather than in general and indiscriminate terms.

Footnotes to Chapter 14

1. M. Wagner and C. Scherzer (trans.), La República de Costa Rica en Centroamérica (San José, Costa Rica: Biblioteca Yorusti, 1944), p. 292.

2. Quoted in Facio, Trayectoria y Crisis de la Federación Centro-americana, op. cit., p. 23.

3. Di Fulvio, op. cit., p. 135; F. S. Parsons and A. De Tuddo, Informe sobre los aspectos técnicos y económicos de la producción de algodón en Centroamérica (FAO/CAIS/58/Rev.1) (Mexico City, March 1959), /mimeographed/, and FAO, Estudio de los aspectos técnicos de la industria ganadera en Centroamérica (FAO/55/7/4320), (Mexico City, 1955), /mimeographed/; Informe sobre los recursos fores-tales y las posibilidades de producción de celulosa y papel en Centro-américa (Mexico City, 1954), /mimeographed/.

4. See United Nations, Economic Commission for Latin America, El Mercado Común de Productos Agropecuarios (E/CN.12/CCE/SC.6/4), p. 2, /mimeographed/.

5. See above, Chapters 3 and 4.

6. United Nations, Economic Commission for Latin America, Los problemas de la política industrial centroamericana, op. cit., pp. 121-2.

7. Multilateral Treaty, Article XXIV; General Treaty, Article XXV, and United Nations, Economic Commission for Latin America, Report of the Central American Economic Co-operation Committee, op. cit., pp. 16-7.

8. United Nations, Economic Commission for Latin America, Evaluación de la Integración Económica en Centroamérica, op. cit., pp. 95-110.

9. Consideration of the question of a possible relationship between the Central American common market and the larger Latin American countries associated in LAFTA has been postponed, on the grounds that it would be premature to establish it before productive activity develops more solid basis in the former. However, larger considerations of a politico-economic nature suggest the advisability of bringing this question to a head at an early date; see below Chapter 15.

10. For more detailed analyses of the problems of foreign investment in the Central American setting, see Permanent Secretariat of the General Treaty on Central American Economic Integration, Nota de la Secretaría sobre Inversiones Extranjeras (Guatemala, 1965), /mimeographed/, and Central American Bank for Economic Integration, Bases para la Formulación de una Política Regional en Materia de Fomento de Inversión (Tegucigalpa, 1965).

CHAPTER **15** ECONOMIC INTEGRATION,
INTERNAL REFORM AND
POLITICAL CHANGE

The Crisis of the Old Order

Economic integration is already a going concern in Central America. As such it cannot escape being influenced by the questions of political development and internal reform which are faced by the five countries. But it can also contribute to the settlement of the issues involved, particularly with respect to the changes in the political systems that will be required for the consolidation of the economic union.

The common market has come into being at a time when the main factors that made for stability in the political systems are undergoing a profound crisis.[1] For several decades the economy, the export economy, has provided productive and remunerative employment to only a part of the increment in the labor force and has failed to provide for appreciable improvements in the levels of living.[2] The demonstration effects of closer contacts with wealthier groups and with richer countries have stirred legitimate ambitions among larger segments of Central American societies. There is now a keener awareness of the contradiction between the formal and the real nature and orientation of the political systems. This gives rise to pressures for a genuinely generalized citizenship.

The ferment for change, occasionally giving rise to violent outbursts, has led to frequent use of the military as the main element for the preservation of order within the status quo in Guatemala, Honduras and El Salvador. Nicaragua has maintained political stability largely on the basis of strong personal rule. In Costa Rica, where firmer democratic institutions had been established at the beginning of this century, the reaction to the first attempts at social reform in the 1940's led thereafter to an even wider dispersion of power. Here political immobilisme has emerged as the natural concomitant of economic stagnation. But, allowing for the differences in political maturity, as well as for local peculiarities, a common denominator can be observed in all the countries: Namely,the relentless operation of new forces undermining the basic coalitions that grew hand in hand with the first stage of Central American development.

Attempts have been made during the last two decades to ensure the continuity of the present systems through legislation on labor, housing, social security, land settlement schemes and public health programs. In general, these measures have had limited application in terms of numbers of people served and the magnitude of the problems involved. Partly for this reason, but also because of the very nature of the measures themselves, being no more than simple income transfers, these attempts have left the systems structurally unchanged, thus failing to get at the roots of the breakdown of the politico-economic order.

The rate of population growth has been rising to more than 3 per cent per annum. Continued crisis in the export economy has led to lower wages and fewer employment opportunities for those working in the coffee industry, while the development of the cotton and livestock industries, with its corresponding enclosure movements, has made deep inroads into the immediate possibilities of providing for the basic needs of families in the subsistence segment of agriculture. The combination of these and other factors is pushing farm people into the cities, where employment opportunities are scarce and wages low, and where their presence makes these insufficiencies more acute, with overcrowding and housing shortages continuing to grow rapidly. Thus, larger and larger groups have come to swell the ranks of those who share little or nothing of the fruits borne by the productive effort of society.

It is from the profound contradiction between increasing aspirations and limited opportunities that the bonds of allegiance to traditional organizations breakdown. It is here that the search for new alternatives begins. Popular or collective movements based on widespread dissatis-faction with the status quo are only the starting point. Whether the present structures are destroyed in an outburst of violence or adjusted to the new requirements in a less drastic fashion, there is the funda-mental need for the excluded majorities to be brought into the system, by making effective their membership in the political going concern through the generalization of economic citizenship. This can be achieved by means of the co-ordinated operations of internal reforms and enlargement of opportunities.

Keeping open the avenues of access to the political system, improving the economic status of urban workers, adjusting tax rates according to progressive criteria,and dispersing widely the ownership of land are the main elements of internal reform. Increasing the efficiency in the traditional lines of export, modernizing domestic agriculture, replacing imports of manufactured goods,and exploiting the resources of the region for the development of new exports spell out the new dimensions of opportunity.

The Facilitating Role of Economic Integration

The political decisions required in each country to reach these objectives will have to contend with the fact of the common market in one way or another. These decisions involve in most cases unilateral measures for action at the national level. In some cases internal reform requires a regional approach; in others, its implementation may be thereby facilitated.

For example, because of the scarcity of land resources relative to population, it is difficult to conceive a national solution of the agrarian question in El Salvador, unless supplemented with measures for the relocation of part of the population of this country throughout the rest of the region. Similarly, it will not be possible to establish the necessary conditions for full mobility of labor between countries until at least part of the very wide disparities in the patterns of income distribution among farm people are removed. Again, the need to establish uniform procedures and legislation among the five countries in matters directly related to the common market could facilitate the simultaneous improvement of national policies in fields such as labor, wage and social security legislation, as well as the tax structure and its administration.[3]

Finally, as was seen in the preceding chapter, the creation of opportunities for growth and improvement of the levels of living of the population, through the expansion of exports, the modernization of domestic agriculture, import substitution,and resource development will have to take place within the framework of economic integration.

Thus, economic integration may provide the context within which internal reforms aid the process of development   in addition to serving the purpose of distributive justice. In turn, integration will face a distributive problem of its own. This consists not only of the distribution of gains and responsibilities among countries, [4] but also of the relative dispersion or concentration of property and opportunity among groups within the common market and the regulation of competition in the industrial sector, as well as policies related to profit margins, wage levels, and social insurance.

The interdependence between internal reform and the creation of new opportunities can make for political development at the regional level. Free trade, tariff equalization, harmonization of fiscal systems, uniform social policies, regional development programs, and agreements to promote the free movement of factors of production are all measures requiring various degrees of political adjustment in each country to the larger interest of the region as a whole. In this way political change grows out of the needs of economic integration. Historical experience in the region shows that it cannot be imposed from above through the establishment of hastily conceived federal institutions. Attempts to re-establish the federal unit at the present time would not only fail in their intended purpose, but could also greatly harm economic integration--the very process that in time might provide the underpinnings for a firm and lasting political organization of regional scope.

The Question of Supra-National Power

Political change at the regional level has the purpose of making the common market a secure enterprise, a dependable vehicle for the five countries to achieve rapid and sustained development. This requires that economic integration and the processes upon which it is built be made independent of the unilateral actions of national governments and of the capricious and arbitrary conduct of individual rulers. Such independence is obtained through the adoption of norms common to all member countries giving rise to co-ordinated, joint and supra-national action.

In creating the common market and establishing the elements of regional policy for its development, the Central American countries have wilfully given up a certain amount of sovereignty. Various functions that the governments used to perform unilaterally, like fixing the height of the tariff on imports or the level and scope of tax exemptions for manufacturing activities, are now subject to multilateral decisions. In other instances, they have agreed to limit the field of national discretion, as in the case of the restraints established upon taxation of Central American goods entering intraregional trade. To this extent, economic integration has resulted already in supra-national action, the probability of its effective application having been increased through the adoption of majority rule as the procedure to be followed by the Executive and Economic Councils in the general case.[5]

Sovereignty has been surrendered within a legal framework--that of the various treaties--by means of which the member countries have attempted to make sure that policies will evolve through joint action and that their directives will be executed at the national level by the national governments.[6] Joint decision-making, based on the common interests of the five countries, therefore, will continue to be crucial as long as there is no federal authority. Moreover, since joint decisions are carried out at the national level, the success of the common market depends mainly upon the willing participation of the member countries.

An important principle thus emerges to which the program should closely adhere in the future, namely that the stronger the commitment at the national level, the more effective and far reaching will the common market be. Governments may in actual practice delegate certain functions to the regional bodies, so that the latter will gradually exercise more power than was conferred upon them by the legal statutes. The growth of supra-national power, to cope with increasingly complex situations going beyond national boundaries within the common market, can and should take place largely by means of this kind of customary practice and development of new functions. But this will take place only if the established bodies of economic integration succeed in the performance of their statutory duties; only as they show that they are efficient mechanisms. Successful performance, therefore, will be the basis for the creation and legitimation of additional degrees of supra-national power.

The purpose of this additional power is not to supplant a strong national participation in the policy-making process, but to shift its execution from the national to the regional level. Developments of this type can already be visualized in fields such as trade policy, customs administration, collection of customs revenues and administration of quarantine regulations.[7] They will require the establishment of new institutions to discharge the corresponding responsibilities. By the nature of the functions involved and the location of their executive aspects outside the national governments, they will bring to the forefront the question of constitutional reform for further economic integration.

Little if anything can be said in this respect before systematic research is done. But it seems fair to assert that, in the same way that giving up national executive power necessitates regional executive organizations, giving up national legislative power must lead to the creation of regional legislative functions and not, as some people believe, to the suppression of those functions.

Development of the Political System

In addition to the political adjustments related with the process of economic integration, there are other aspects having to do with the intrinsic purposes of the political system itself and with its development under the conditions prevailing in Central America. It should be remembered, in this connection, that in this region, as well as in the rest of Latin Americas, independence from colonial rule was achieved within an ideal of liberty and democracy. The fact that this ideal has not been fulfilled so far does not mean in any way that it will now be given up in the name of a high rate of economic growth. On the contrary, the question here must be framed in terms of how the achievement of freedom and democracy can lead to rapid and sustained development and how economic integration can contribute to these ends.

In clarifying these relationships it seems that much confusion would be avoided if it were acknowledged from the outset that liberty and democracy are not necessarily related only to the instrumentalities that the people in the United States and Western Europe have devised for their achievement. One hundred years ago the Central Americans borrowed the political ideas of American, British and French liberalism and tried to apply them without any assimilation or adaptation to local social and economic conditions. Time has shown that instruments such as separation of powers, periodic change in the executive branch and the organization of people in a variety of political parties have had serious centrifugal effects, threatening the very possibilities of survival of the political system or paralyzing its actions.

Experience reflects the continued presence of strong personal elements in its operations and the existence of large groups outside the system itself. This is true not only of Central America but more generally of developing nations. Thus it is not a simple coincidence that, within the formal apparatus of political democracy, the substantive business of government is often conducted through an all-powerful executive and a single political party of wide spectrum. That this is the case in countries which are only beginning to join the community of nations, or which are emerging out of a total political upheaval, is understandable. But that it should also be the case of countries whom have been trying the instruments of North American and European democracy for a long time without much success, reflects the sterility of political theory during the last two centuries.

Central America cannot expect to be isolated in these troubled times of cold war and ideological cleavage; but within the larger framework of international affairs, she should be able at least to formulate her own solutions, tailored to her own conditions. In this way, the field is left open for political innovation within the limits defined by the general ideas of liberty and democracy, the needs of economic growth and a fundamental concern to develop a decentralized system of organization.

By a decentralized system is meant here one where decision-making is widely scattered throughout and public action, in addition to the direct provision of services, proceeds in terms of rules defining by way of exclusion the lawful limits of human behavior. There is an obvious relationship between a system of this type and political liberty; there is another one between it and the efficiency with which economic growth is to be achieved. This is why so much emphasis has been placed throughout this study upon the need to visualize many of the actions of government in terms of working rules, procedures, incentives and disincentives which are made to intervene between the emergence of economic problems and their solution, as reflected in the actual performance of the economy.

Evidently, if by virtue of a severe breakdown, a system is facing not the questions of liberty and economic growth but the more elementary function of surviving as a going concern, no matter how precariously it may be put together at a given time, then it may have to do so by means of a tight centralization of the decision-making process. But once it reaches the minimum conditions of survival, the question arises as to whether a high degree of centralization is compatible with political liberty and economic development.

It should be clear also that public and private property are not necessarily synonymous with a centralized and a decentralized system, respectively, but with the way in which the systems operate. In this case, however, the Central American countries have a basic commitment to develop a strong private economy and to place upon it a large responsibility for their economic growth. Thus it may be possible for the governments to keep their activities within manageable proportions, while private enterprise--ranging from corporate organizations, to family farms, family industrial plants, mixed private-public firms and co-operatives--attempts in the same manner to do its part of the job. Given the present picture of total capabilities, the governments could not proceed otherwise without facing almost impossible tasks. It is important to be aware of this, so that the countries can get on with the construction of a working partnership between the public and the private sectors, without which development cannot take place.

It does not follow that a decentralized system leads either to the absence of government over large areas of endeavor or to the existence of a weak government. On the contrary, there is great need for a strong government in times of profound change, if only to maintain the going concern of organized society. This is the strength that grows out of bringing the large groups of excluded people into the system. Then a wedge is driven between the structures of political and of economic power and the government ceases to reflect merely the interests of those who have a stake in the status quo.

The substantive content of the relationship of the state to the economy may differ also in Central America from that which has been developed in other countries. The differences are rooted in both the peculiarities of the region's historical evolution and the needs of its economic growth. The specific nature of this relationship cannot be anticipated now; but the need to cope with much larger internal and external inequalities, the tradition of government assistance in the fulfillment of private ends,and the unwillingness to accept private concentrations of economic power of magnitudes similar to those prevailing in some of the more advanced countries,assert themselves as three factors that would tend to make for a different kind of substantive connection between the state and the economy.

Economic Integration and the Emergence of New Political Structures

Political and economic change through institutional adjustment becomes more difficult and sometimes impossible within a stagnant framework of opportunity. That is why economic integration looms so large in this context. For, in establishing the common market the

Central American countries have created a new vector of opportunity along which national institutions will be reoriented and additional centers of decision-making set up at the regional level. Depending on the way in which this is done, economic integration may make for political development, facilitating the reconstruction required by the national systems for their continued stability.

It is useful to note, for example, how the need for certain national actions to obtain regional approval, in spite of "log-rolling," provides an opportunity to eliminate arbitrary behavior and to transcend the narrow structures of traditional vested interests. It seems that this is a better way to achieve improvement than by attempting to force de facto, arbitrary governments out of existence through the shallow approach of righteous indignation at the apparent or real violations of the principles of a democracy for which the required bases are lacking.

This undesirable kind of government will go out of the Central American scene as the evolution of political and economic conditions succeeds in establishing the necessary bases, not before. In this connection, it is important to be aware of the need to leave the questions of governmental changes entirely in the hands of the people in each country and to make sure that the business of integration is smoothly conducted by the five common market members in spite of the discontinuities brought about by those changes.

The connection between economic integration and political development will be established with the emergence of a new public. This public will be made up of the persons, groups and interests for whom economic integration is acquiring increasing importance and which require the development of safe and dependable norms and procedures at the regional level. For in the long run it is possible to visualize new political alignments, different from those that charac-terized these countries during their first stage of development.

Industrial entrepreneurs have not yet differentiated themselves as a group from the traditional agricultural exporters; nor have the industrial workers and the middle classes realized how closely associated their interests are with those of the agricultural workers and subsistence farmers. Some time, perhaps a long time, will have to elapse before these hurdles are overcome. But, to the extent that the internal market remains as a limiting factor and that the workings of the domestic economy grow in relative importance and its various sectors become increasingly interdependent, conditions will develop for a great coalition of these groups to come into being and to take its place among the main underpinnings of the political system.

It would be a mistake to assume that this process will occur without difficulty. Being both political and economic in nature, it will evolve in the thick and thin of conflict, as divergent interests clash. In fact, there is no assurance that it will be possible to manage these conflicts in such a way as to avoid a breakdown of the ongoing systems. Two intimately related orientations may be useful in any attempt to make this possible. There is the need to abandon a certain moralistic approach to the problems of development, in which it is sometimes difficult to know whether the objective of policy is that of making the required adjustments and the necessary efforts to achieve rapid and sustained growth, or whether the purpose is rather that of physically wiping out the dominant groups of the present. It would then be possible to approach these problems with the explicit acknowledgement that what is required is not to transcend the lines of political and economic groupings and to create solidarity where previously there were conflicting interests, but to develop a capacity for them to coexist, to live and work together and to grow as the system grows, sharing equitably of its fruits.

Footnotes to Chapter 15

1. This refers to their organic stability and not to the more superficial phenomenon of "revolution within the palace" which usually leaves the system intact.

2. See above, Chapter 6.

3. United Nations, Economic Commission for Latin America, Report of the Central American Economic Co-operation Committee, Sixth Meeting (E/CN.12/533), op. cit., p. 22.

4. See above, Chapter 13.

5. General Treaty, Article XXI.

6. In the cases of the Central American Bank of Economic Integration and ICAITI policy is executed at the regional level, but the services performed by these institutions do not involve the surrender of sovereignty.

7. See above, Chapters 12 and 14. See also General Treaty, Article I and United Nations, Economic Commission for Latin America, Report of the Central American Economic Co-operation Committee (E/CN.12/672), op. cit., p. 16.

BIBLIOGRAPHY

Official Documents

Banco Central de Nicaragua. Primer Informe Anual, 1961. Managua, Nicaragua.

Banco Central de Reserva. Acuerdo para el Establecimiento de una Unión Monetaria Centroamericana. San Salvador, 1964. (Mimeographed.)

Banco Centroamericano de Integración Económica. Bases para la Formulación de una Política Regional en Materia de Fomento de Inversiones. Tegucigalpa, Honduras, 1965.

_____. Primera Memoria Anual, 1961-62. Tegucigalpa, Honduras, 1962.

Banco Nacional de Comercio Exterior. La Integración Económica Latinoamericana. Mexico City, 1963.

Central American Research Institute for Industry. ICAITI as a United Nations Special Fund Project: Request for a Reinforced Extension of the Project for the Period July 1, 1965 to June 30, 1968. Guatemala, November 1964. (Ditto.)

Choussy, Félix. Actual Panorama Económico Agrícola de El Salvador. San Salvador: Ministry of Agriculture, 1952.

Contratos Celebrados entre el Gobierno de Honduras y la Cuyamel Fruit Company y la Tela Railroad Company. Tegucigalpa, Honduras: Central Bank's Library. (Mimeographed.)

East Africa, Report of the Economic and Fiscal Commission. London: Her Majesty's Stationary Office (Comnd. 1279), 1961.

Escuela Superior de Administración Pública América Central (ESAPAC).
    Report of the Director to the Board. San José, Costa Rica,
    November 1963.

Herrarte, Alberto. Documentos de la Unión Centroamericana.
    Guatemala: Editorial del Ministerio de Educación Pública, 1957.

International Bank for Reconstruction and Development and Inter-
    national Development Association. The Commodity Problems.
    Report No. EG-129, Staff Study of the Economic Department.
    Washington, D. C., May 1964.

Organization of Central American States (ODECA). Acta de la
    Primera Reunión de Ministros de Trabajo y Previsión Social de
    Centroamérica. San Salvador, 1954.

Permanent Secretariat of the General Treaty for Central American
    Economic Integration (SIECA). Annual Report, 1963-64.
    Guatemala, 1965.

_____. Informe de la Primera Reunión de Ministros de Agricultura
    (SIECA/RMA-I/33). Guatemala, 1964.

_____. Informe de la Reunión de Institutos de Fomento y Estabili-
    zación de Precios (SIECA/IFE-IV/D.6). Guatemala, 1964.

_____. Informe de la Reunión de Ministros de Economía y Obras
    Públicas de Centroamérica (SIECA/MEOP-1/2). Guatemala,
    1963.

_____. Informe de la Tercera Reunión de la Comisión Centroame-
    ricana de Telecomunicaciones (SIECA/CCT-III/3). San Salvador,
    1964.

_____. Los granos básicos en Centroamérica y Panamá
    (SIECA/IFE-IV/DI.2). Guatemala, 1963.

_____. Nota de la Secretaría sobre Inversiones Extranjeras.
    Guatemala, 1965.

_____. Tercer Compendio Estadístico Centroamericano.
    Guatemala, 1963.

Ramm-Ericson, Nils. Restrictions Affecting the Interterritorial Trade
between Kenya, Tanzania and Uganda. A memorandum prepared
for the Economic Division of the Treasury, East African Common
Services Organization (EACSO). Nairobi, 1966.
(Mimeographed.)

Roberts, Ralph J. and Irving, Earl M. Mineral Deposits of Central
America. Washington, D. C.: U. S. Department of the
Interior, 1957.

United Nations. Report of the Mission to Study ICAITI. New York,
1963.

United Nations, Economic Commission for Latin America. América
Latina y la Conferencia de las Naciones Unidas sobre Comercio
y Desarrollo (E/CN.12/693). Santiago, Chile, 1964.
(Mimeographed.)

_____. Análisis y Proyecciones del Desarrollo Económico IX.
El Desarrollo Económico de Nicaragua (E/CN.12/712).
Mexico City, 1965   (Mimeographed.)

_____. Análisis y Proyecciones del Desarrollo Económico XI.
El Desarrollo Económico de Honduras (E/CN.12/549).
Mexico City, 1960.

_____. Annual Report, 1964-65 (E/CN.12/731/Rev. 2).
New York, 1965.

_____. Convenios Centroamericanos de Integración Económica
(E/CN.12/CCE/315). Mexico City, 1964. (Mimeographed.)

_____. Desarrollo Combinado de los Sistemas Centrales de
El Salvador y Honduras (E/CN.12/CCE/SC.5/11). Mexico
City, 1963. (Mimeographed.)

_____. Desarrollo Combinado del Sistema Pacífico de Nicaragua
y del Sistema Central de Costa Rica (E/CN.12/CCE/SC.5/31).
Mexico City, 1964. (Mimeographed.)

_____. Documentación del Comité de Cooperación Económica del
Istmo Centroamericano. CEPAL/MEX/65/5. Mexico City, 1965.
(Mimeographed.)

_____ . Economic Bulletins for Latin America: "The International Banana Market - Its Evolution and Prospects," "The Central American Economic Integration Programme," "General Situation and Future Outlook of the Central American Economic Integration Programme," "Central America: Industrial Policy Problems." New York, 1958, 1959, 1963, 1964.

_____ . Economic Surveys of Latin America. New York, 1949. 1953, 1963.

_____ . El Mercado Común de Productos Agropecuarios (E/CN.12/CCE/SC.6/4). Mexico City, 1964. (Mimeographed.)

_____ . El Programa de Integración Económica de Centroamérica y el Tratado de Asociación Económica Suscrito por El Salvador, Guatemala y Honduras. Interrelaciones y Posibles Formas de Consolidar y Acelerar la Integración Económica del Istmo (E/CN.12/CCE/212). Mexico City, 1960. (Mimeographed.)

_____ . El Sector Externo y el Desarrollo Económico de Centroamérica, 1950-62 (CCE/SC.1/R. Ex. 1/DI.2). Mexico City, 1964. (Mimeographed.)

_____ . Evaluación de la Integración Económica en Centroamérica (E/CN.12/CCE/327/Rev. 1). Mexico City, 1966. (Mimeographed.)

_____ . Foreign Capital in Latin America. New York, 1955.

_____ . Informe de la Duodécima Reunión del Subcomité de Comercio Centroamericano (E/CN.12/CCE/247). Mexico City, 1962. (Mimeographed.)

_____ . Informe de la Reunión de Funcionarios Centroamericanos de Electrificación (E/CN.12/CCE/107). Mexico City, 1957. (Mimeographed.)

_____ . Informe de la Reunión del Grupo de Trabajo sobre Interconexión Eléctrica Nicaragua y Costa Rica (E/CN.12/CCE/SC.5/32). Mexico City, 1964. (Mimeographed.)

_____ . Informe de la Primera Reunión del Subcomité Centroamericano de Electrificación (E/CN.12/CCE/SC.5/4). Mexico City, 1959. (Mimeographed.)

_____ . Informe de la Segunda Reunión del Subcomité Centroamericano de Electrificación (E/CN.12/CCE/306). Mexico City, 1963. (Mimeographed.)

_____ . Informe de la Segunda Reunión del Subcomité Centroamericano de Transportes (E/CN.12/CCE/307). Mexico City, 1963. (Mimeographed.)

_____ . Informe de la Primera Reunión del Comité de Cooperación Económica del Istmo Centroamericano (E/CN.12/AC.17/24). Tegucigalpa, Honduras, 1952. (Mimeographed.)

_____ . Informe sobre el Tercer Período de Sesiones de la Comisión Económica para América Latina (E/1717). New York, 1949.

_____ . La Economía de América Latina en 1965. Santiago, Chile, 1966.

_____ . La Política Regional de la Energía en Centroamérica (E/CN.12/CCE/SC.5/41). Mexico City, 1966. (Mimeographed.)

_____ . La Politica Tributaria y el Desarrollo Económico en Centroamérica (E/CN.12/486). Mexico City, 1956.

_____ . Los Problemas de la Política Industrial Centroamericana (E/CN.12/CCE/311). Mexico City, 1964. (Mimeographed.)

_____ . Nomenclatura Arancelaria Uniforme Centroamericana (NAUCA) y su Manual de Codificación (E/CN.12/420). New York, 1955.

_____ . Preliminary Report by the Executive Secretary on Economic Integration and Reciprocity in Central America (E/CN.12/AC.17/3). Mexico City, 1952. (Mimeographed.)

_____ . Programa de Desarrollo de la Industria de Hilados y Tejidos de Algodón en Centroamérica (E/CN.12/CCE/356). Mexico City, 1956. (Mimeographed.)

_____ . Reports of the Central American Economic Co-operation Committee: Sixth Session (E/CN.12/533), Seventh Session (E/CN.12/552), Eighth Session and Third and Fourth Special Sessions (E/CN.12/672) and Ninth Session (E/CN.12/752). New York, 1960, 1961, 1964, 1966.

_____ . Report of the Economic Commission for Latin America, Fourth Session (E/2021), New York, 1951.

_____ . The Economic Development of Latin America and Its Principal Problems (E/CN.12/89), New York, 1950.

United Nations Food and Agriculture Organization (FAO). Boletín Mensual de Economía y Estadística Agrícola. "Evolución y Estructura del Mercado Bananero Mundial." Rome, February 1959.

_____ . Estudio de los Aspectos Técnicos de la Industria Ganadera en Centroamérica (FAO/55/7/4320). Mexico City, 1957. (Mimeographed.)

_____ . Informe sobre los Aspectos Agrícolas, Técnicos y Económicos de la Producción de Algodón en Centroamérica (FAO/CAIS/58/Rev.1). Mexico City, 1959.

_____ . Informe sobre los Recursos Forestales y las Posibilidades de Producción de Celulosa y Papel en Centroamérica. Mexico City, 1954. (Mimeographed.)

_____ . La Economía Mundial del Café. Serie sobre Productos No. 33. Rome, 1961.

United Nations Special Fund. Estudio sobre la Red Regional de Telecomunicaciones entre las Repúblicas del Istmo Centroamericano. Nueva York, 1964.

United States Department of Commerce. United States Investments in the Latin American Economy. Washington, D. C.: Government Printing Office, 1957.

Books

Anguilé, André G. and David, Jacques E. L'Afrique sans frontières. Monaco (Pté.): Societé des Editions Paul Bory, 1965.

Balassa, Bela. The Theory of Economic Integration. London: George Allen and Unwind Ltd., 1961.

Bitter, W. Die Wirtschftliche Eraberung Mittelamerikas durch die Bananen, Trustorganisation und imperialistische Bedeutung der United Fruit Company. Hamburg: G. Wasterman, 1921.

Baranyai, L. and Mills, J. C. Convenios de Estabilización de las Materias Primas. Mexico City: CEMLA, 1962.

Cabrales, Luis Alberto. Historia de Nicaragua. Managua, 1961.

Carr, Albert Z. The World and William Walker. New York: Harper and Row, 1963.

Commons, John R. Legal Foundations of Capitalism. Madison: The University of Wisconsin Press, 1959.

De León Aragón, Oscar. Los Contratos de la United Fruit Company y las Compañías Muelleras de Guatemala. Guatemala: Editorial del Ministerio de Educación Pública, 1950.

Dell, Sidney. Trade Blocks and Common Markets. London: Constable, 1963.

Di Fulvio, Antonio. El Café en el Mundo. Rome: Instituto Internacional de Agricultura, 1947.

Facio, Rodrigo. Estudio sobre Economía Costarricense, San José, Costa Rica: Editorial Surco, 1942.

_____. La Moneda y la Banca Central en Costa Rica, Mexico City: Fondo de Cultura Económica, 1947.

_____. Trayectoria y Crisis de la Federación Centroamericana, San José, Costa Rica: Imprenta Nacional, 1949.

Frank, Isaiah. The European Common Market: An Analysis of Commercial Policy. New York: Frederick A. Praeger, Inc. Publishers, 1961.

Furnivall, J. S. Colonial Policy and Practice. Cambridge: Cambridge University Press, 1948.

Furtado, Celso. Formación Económica del Brasil. Mexico City: Fondo de Cultura Económica, 1962.

Guerra y Sánchez, Ramiro. Sugar and Society in the Caribbean. New Haven: Yale University Press, 1964.

Guier, Enrique. El General Morazán. San José, Costa Rica: Imprenta Lehmann, 1962.

Karnes, Thomas L. The Failure of Union: Central America 1824-1960. Chapel Hill, N. C.: The University of North Carolina Press, 1961.

Malavassi, Carmen S. de and André S., Belén. El Café en la Historia de Costa Rica. San José: Universidad de Costa Rica, 1958. (Mimeographed.)

May, Stacy and Plaza, Galo. La United Fruit Company en América Latina. Mexico City: National Planning Association, 1959.

Meade, J. E. Problems of Economic Union. Chicago: The University of Chicago Press, 1953.

Monterrey, Francisco J. Historia de El Salvador, Anotaciones Cronológicas 1810-71. San Salvador, 1943.

Nurkse, Ragnar. Problems of Capital Formation in Underdeveloped Countries. Oxford: Basil Blackwell, 1953.

Obregón Loría, Rafael. La Campaña del Tránsito. San José, Costa Rica: Editorial Universitaria, 1956.

Robinson, E. A. (ed.). Economic Consequences of the Size of Nations. Proceedings of the Conference held by the International Economic Association. London: MacMillan & Co. Ltd., 1960.

Rochac, Alfonso. Evolución Monetaria Salvadoreña, Tres Ensayos sobre Historia Monetaria. San Salvador: Universidad de El Salvador, 1961.

Sáenz, Vicente. Nuestras Vías Interoceánicas. Mexico City: Editorial América Nueva, 1957.

Salazar, José Manuel. Tierras y Colonización en Costa Rica. Serie Tesis de Grado No. 15. San José: Publicaciones de la Universidad de Costa Rica, 1962.

Sannwald, R. F. and Stohler, J. Economic Integration: Theoretical Assumptions and Consequences of European Integration. Princeton, N. J.: Princeton University Press, 1959.

Soley Güell, Tomás. Historia Económica y Hacendaria de Costa Rica. San José: Editorial Universitaria, 1947.

Solórzano Fernández, Valentín. Historia de la Evolución Económica de Guatemala. Mexico City, 1947.

Stokes, William S. Honduras: An Area Study in Government. Madison: The University of Wisconsin Press, 1950.

Toppel, Johannes. Die Banane Chemisch. Berlin: Technischer Verlag der Bodenbinder, 1935.

Torres, Abelardo. Evolución de las Ideas Liberales en las Instituciones Políticas y Jurídicas de la República Federal de Centroamérica y del Estado de El Salvador. San Salvador: Universidad de El Salvador, 1951.

Viner, J. The Customs Union Issue. New York: Carnegie Endowment for International Peace, 1950.

Wagner, M. and Scherzer, O. (trans.). La República de Costa Rica en Centroamérica. San José: Biblioteca Yorusti, 1944.

Wallich, Henry C. and Adler, John H. Proyecciones Económicas de las Finanzas Públicas: Un Estudio Experimental en El Salvador. Mexico City: Fondo de Cultura Económica, 1949.

Wells, William V. Explorations and Adventures in Honduras. New
    York: Harper and Brothers, 1857.

Young, John Parke. Central American Currency and Finance.
    Princeton, N. J.: Princeton University Press, 1825.

Articles

Castillo, Carlos M. "La Agricultura Tradicional en una Economía en
    Desarrollo," El Trimestre Económico, Vol. XXX (4), No. 120.
    Mexico City: Fondo de Cultura Económica, 1963.

_____. "Problemas Políticos y Administrativos del Desarrollo Eco-
    nómico," El Trimestre Económico, Vol. XXVI (1), No. 101.
    Mexico City: Fondo de Cultura Económica, 1960.

Kaldor, Nicholas. "Problemas Económicos de Chile," El Trimestre
    Económico, Vol. XXVI (2), No. 102. Mexico City: Fondo de
    Cultura Económica, 1960.

Lewis, W. A. "Economic Development with Unlimited Supplies of
    Labor," The Manchester School of Economic and Social Studies,
    Vol. XXII, No. 2. Manchester, 1954.

Rostow, Walt W. "Agriculture's Role in Economic Development,"
    Foreign Agriculture, Vol. I, No. 35. Washington, D. C.,
    1963.

Wolf, Eric R. and Mintz, Sidney W. "Haciendas and Plantations in
    Middle America and the Antilles," Social and Economic
    Studies. Jamaica: University College of the West Indies,
    Institute of Social and Economic Research, 1957.

ABOUT THE AUTHOR

Dr. Carlos M. Castillo is a Costa Rican national and has been an official of the United Nations since 1956. During this period he has worked mainly in the Central American economic integration program, at the Mexico Office of the Economic Commission for Latin America, where he has held the posts of Chief, Agricultural Economics Section (1956-58); Secretary of the Central American Economic Co-operation Committee (1959-60); Deputy Director (1961-62), and Director (1963-66). More recently, the five Central American Governments appointed him Executive Secretary of the General Treaty on Economic Integration for a three year period beginning in October, 1966.

Dr. Castillo received his Master's degree in economics at the University of Tennessee (1953) and the Ph.D. degree at the University of Wisconsin (1965). Before joining the United Nations he worked for the Inter-American Institute of Agricultural Sciences (1953-55) and has been associated for brief periods with the University of Chicago (1960) as Research Associate and with the University of Wisconsin (1964) as Consultant to the Land Tenure Center. He is now a member of the Research Advisory Committee of this Center, as well as adviser to the Mexican Center of Agrarian Research. He is also a member of the International Conference of Agricultural Economists.

Dr. Castillo's written work includes articles in professional journals and other publications on the institutional and organizational aspects of agricultural development and on the theory and practice of multinational economic integration. He has participated in numerous international meetings dealing with problems in both fields. Early in 1966 he worked as a consultant to the Commission on East African Co-operation.